Absent Friend

A meditation on a friendship with Leonard Cohen

John MacKenna

The Harvest Press

Absent Friend
John MacKenna
Published in 2023
The Harvest Press

www.theharvestpress.ie

ISBN 978-1-8380836-7-0

Cover illustration: Lucy Deegan
Cover design: Faye Tucker

A Note on the Author

John MacKenna is the author of twenty-three books – novels, short-story collections, memoir, poetry and biography – and a number of stage and radio plays. He is a winner of *The Irish Times*, Hennessy and Cecil Day-Lewis Awards. He is also a winner of a Jacob's Radio award for his documentary series on Leonard Cohen and a Worldplay Silver Medal (New York) for his radio play *The Woman at the Window* (RTE Radio 1). He teaches creative writing at Maynooth University and at The Hedge School on the Moone.

Also by John MacKenna

Novels
Clare
The Last Fine Summer
A Haunted Heart
The Space Between Us
Joseph
Hold Me Now

Short-Story Collections
The Fallen and Other Stories
A Year of Our Lives
The River Field
Once We Sang Like Other Men
We Seldom Talk About the Past

Memoir
Things You Should Know

Non-Fiction
Castledermot and Kilkea: A Social History
Shackleton: An Irishman in Antarctica (with Jonathan Shackleton)
The Lost Village
I Knew This Place (Radio Essays)

Children's Books
Turkey's Delight
South

Poetry Collections
The Occasional Optimist
Ten Poems
Where Sadness Begins
By the Light of Four Moons

Plays
The Fallen
Who by Fire
The Unclouded Day
Towards Evening
Faint Voices
Sergeant Pepper
Over the Rainbow
The Woman at the Window
My Father's Life
Redemption Song
Lucinda Sly
Between Your Love and Mine (with Leonard Cohen)
The Mental

For Angela.

Thanks for walking the road with me.

One

It began, as things often do, in an oblique way in the summer of 1971. I'd just finished my first year in college and our neighbour, Kevin Kelly, had given me a holiday job. It was my initial outing as a builder's labourer.

I'd managed to get through the first week without killing or being killed and, on the Friday night, I'd borrowed my father's car and driven to visit a girlfriend who lived twenty-five miles away. It was a warm, blue-sky evening and we sat on a wall in a field near her house, shooting the breeze and making plans.

'Are you ok?' she asked.

'Why?'

'You look pale.'

'I've got a headache,' I said. 'I'm not feeling great.'

'You should get home. You really do look pale.'

She walked me to the car and I began the drive home. By the time I'd driven four miles, the road and trees and ditches were swimming, the light from the evening sun was glaring in my eyes and I slowed the car, uncertain about where I was or how close I was to other cars. Somehow, I made it home and into bed and that's, more or less, all I remember for a couple of weeks.

~

There were odd moments when I surfaced from the darkness: to hear our GP saying he didn't think it would be wise to move me to hospital; to sense the local curate applying oil to my forehead and intoning the prayers for the dying; to see my father hanging blackout curtains in the window.

And then two weeks had passed and I began to emerge from the darkness. The blackouts were taken down. The GP said things were looking better. My mother mentioned the word meningitis. I became aware of the phone ringing downstairs and messages were conveyed from the girl I'd been visiting.

My sister, Dolores, brought the record player up from the sitting room and put it on a table at my bedside. Her friend, Margaret Leahy, loaned me two albums: *Songs of Leonard Cohen* and *Songs from a Room*. And so began an expedition that would last two lifetimes.

At that stage, I was only vaguely aware of Leonard Cohen's music, having heard 'So Long Marianne' and 'Suzanne' on the radio. Beyond that, I knew nothing of the man and was unaware of the fact that he had written novels and poetry; his work and his sometimes troubled and troubling life were, effectively, unknown to me.

~

I began by listening to Leonard's second album, *Songs from a Room*.

It was like nothing I'd ever heard before. The charts at the time were filled with pop songs that ranged from Middle of the Road to Rod Stewart to Paul McCartney to T Rex to The Tams, Lobo, Mungo Jerry and Buffy Sainte Marie. But there was nothing there to prepare me for the sounds I was hearing in my bedroom.

From the first notes of 'Bird on the Wire' with its tantalising but recognisable imagery of midnight drunks in a choir (they were a constant at Christmas midnight Mass in Castledermot) to the women in their darkened doors (I'd seen them on the docks in my schooldays in Limerick and along the canal banks in Dublin) through 'Story of Isaac' which took a biblical tale with which I was long familiar and turned the narrative on its head by retelling or freshly telling it in the voice of the nine-year-old Isaac. Thanks to a brilliant English teacher, Ray Kearns, I had begun writing in secondary school but this was a new way of seeing and hearing a familiar tale. It opened my eyes to the possibilities of retelling old stories in a fresh way and unbolted another doorway into literature.

The conciseness of Leonard's imagery was a source of inspiration and something that would stay with me through my writing life. He didn't spend a verse explaining how high up the mountain Isaac and

Abraham were; Isaac simply remembered his father throwing a bottle over the edge of a precipice and hearing it break a minute later. That told me everything I needed to know and located the pair on the mountain side.

But the gift wasn't simply in the writing; it was there, too, in the phrasing and delivery of a story and it was manifest in Cohen's reading of the Anna Marly/Hy Zaret song 'The Partisan.' I had come close to death in the previous weeks but there was something soothing in the cadence and something strangely reassuring in the image of the wind blowing through the graves in his performance of the song. And there it was, again, the beautiful conciseness, the old woman dying 'without a word.'

This wasn't just a new musical landscape; it was a new world. The images were erudite; the voice was unlike anything I'd heard; the music was deceptively simple. Suddenly, I had discovered someone whose sentiments in some way mirrored my own. In 'Tonight Will Be Fine' Cohen sang of choosing the rooms he lived in carefully, of their simplicity, of his beloved undressing for him – these were the aspirations of the young and relatively naive man I was. I'd just spent a year in digs in Dublin, carefully overseen by my landlady who'd become an unexpected surrogate mother. The possibilities of a place of my own and the freedoms that might bring were being sung in my ears as I listened to the closing track on the album. I had been critically ill but now I was on the mend and I wanted, more than ever, to live and be alive to the pleasures of existence. And here was a songwriter who'd been reading not just my diary but my mind as well.

Songs of Leonard Cohen didn't find its way onto the record deck for several days and, when it did, the track I kept replacing the stylus on was track two on side two, 'Hey That's No Way to Say Goodbye.' There must have been a sense of divination in that choice because, by summer's end, the girlfriend I had gone to visit on that night when I became ill had found another boyfriend – ironically, a handsome, young, guitar-playing Canadian. The fact became obvious at a summer barbecue on an August evening and the drive home from that was hampered, again, by poor eyesight but, on this occasion, brought on by a wave of self-pity.

But there was a consolation. I might have lost the girl but I had the music (I hadn't even heard 'Chelsea Hotel' at that stage) and I was hooked on the extraordinary work of this poet.

Two

Leonard's third album, *Songs of Love and Hate*, had been released in March 1971 and, when I got back to Dublin, in the October of that year, I bought a copy. I had a weekly fund at the time, to cover bus-fares and lunches but, in those days, hopping on and off the open backed buses was not difficult and, anyway, I liked walking. So, every Friday I bought an LP for £1/17/6, mostly in George Murray's record shop on Grafton St. where, by the end of my first year in college, George and I were on first name terms. Occasionally, in search of something obscure, I'd find my way to Disc Finder on Baggot St.

With *Songs of Love and Hate*, I was in for a surprise. The work was unlike anything on the first two LPs. Someone described it as one of the most frightening albums they'd ever heard and I was mesmerised by the sound, unsettled by the darkness, intrigued by the writing and tensely engrossed in what I was hearing. From the first glimpse of the album cover there was no escape and from the opening words of 'Avalanche' the darkness descended.

The song, like the title, swept me along, bleak and twisted and relentless. 'Last Year's Man' and 'Dress Rehearsal Rag' were equally hypnotic and only the lift in the music of 'Diamonds in the Mine,' which closed side one, allowed me room to catch my breath while I absorbed the fact – one I had almost accepted, at the age of eighteen – that the world is sometimes an entirely forlorn and unforgiving place.

I clearly remember listening to the album in the sitting room of my digs at 133 Booterstown Avenue. The afternoon was bright and sunny, the October trees throwing their yellow leaf-light through the window. But, as I turned the album and eavesdropped on side two, I was somewhere else. And the songs which transported me were 'Famous Blue Raincoat' and the magnificent 'Joan of Arc.'

With Joan, Leonard had done what he had done with Isaac. He had taken a figure from history, a figure of which I'd no more than a passing knowledge, though I was a history student, and turned a fresh and captivating eye on her and her story. He had given her a voice, had softened a mythical figure and allowed me to see and sense the feelings and failings and fears a young woman might well have gone through.

~

March 18, 1972. I was in my second year in college and Leonard Cohen was playing at the National Boxing Stadium on the South Circular Road in Dublin and I had a ticket to the early show, the first of two. Concerts were concerts back then. I don't think the word gig had entered my vocabulary.

This would be my second ever proper student concert. The first had been The Freshmen's *Peace on Earth* performance at the RDS in Dublin in November 1970. I'd attended that with my friend Pat Clowry. Hilton Edwards, replacing the indisposed Micheál Mac Liammóir, had intoned the readings between the songs. It was a strikingly dignified and musically exquisite performance in the staid surroundings of the RDS.

~

The National Stadium was an entirely different kind of venue. Built in 1939, by the seventies, it had its own shabby, down-at-heel atmosphere that reeked with the echoes of the musicians who had played there – from Genesis to Led Zeppelin to The Who. For me, as a teenager stepping through its doorway for the first time, it was a magical place where anything was possible.

I sat enthralled through Leonard's initial performance. He began with 'So Long Marianne' and moved into 'Bird on the Wire.' The fourth song he sang that night was 'Kevin Barry.' It brought the house down. Leonard introduced the song by clarifying that he didn't 'wish to burden you here with another war, another cause, but there are struggles in other places and they all amount to the same thing; that is, men of eighteen and nineteen getting killed and this is one from Ireland.'

This was 1972, the conflict in Northern Ireland was escalating – by the end of the year, four hundred and seventy-nine people would have been killed.

I was involved in the Official Republican movement at the time but I was struck by Leonard's phrase 'getting killed.' It was a far cry from my romantic notion of a heroic death.

A couple of songs later he sang another cover, 'The Partisan' and then a third, a song I'd never heard before, Richard Blakeslee's astonishing and moving 'Passing Through.' The song (from the London recording of that tour) would appear in 1973 on the *Live Songs* album. To my delight, 'Hey that's No Way to Say Goodbye' made an appearance close to the end of the show and the concert concluded with another unexpected song. Leonard prefaced it by saying: 'There's so much dogmatic information about who you should be and what you should be and a long time ago somebody wrote this song …' and then he quietly moved into a laid-back version of 'As Time Goes By.'

With that, the show was over. The audience began to leave the National Stadium, making way for the incoming enthusiasts who were already queueing for the second performance of the evening.

~

More than anything, I wanted to see and hear Leonard again. To relive the exhilaration I'd just been through. There were no guarantees about the future, much less about Leonard Cohen ever returning to this island.

I hung about inside the stadium door, wondering how I could wheedle my way into remaining for the second show and then, like an angel of the Lord, a fellow-student at UCD, Luigi Rea, appeared from behind one of the catering wagons. His parents' company were doing the in-house catering for both shows. I explained my predicament and in a couple of minutes I had been seconded onto their staff and got to see Leonard a second time, from my place at the side of the catering kiosk.

Three

In the student years that followed, Leonard's albums travelled with me through flats in Sandymount and Leinster Square and Palmerston Road; through exam preparations and summer jobs and graduation. In Sandymount, the young Englishwoman who lived downstairs and who sometimes borrowed milk or sugar from me would comment on the fact that the music she heard from my flat was much quieter than the music played by the previous tenant.

'You're into Leonard Cohen, he was into Led Zeppelin. I prefer your stuff,' she told me one evening.

I offered to loan her one or two of the albums.

'Better not,' she said. 'I could be gone in a couple of weeks …or days.'

A few years later, I would read about her murder in a newspaper – killed by her pimp.

~

By the time *New Skin for the Old Ceremony* was released I'd completed college and was working for the summer in the Hallmark Cards factory in Templeogue with my friend Richard Ball. We shared a tiny bedsit on Palmerston Road. It was half a room really, with the result that we could smell and hear what the man in the next door flat was cooking, through the leaf-thin wall. We spent evenings poring over the lyrics of 'Chelsea Hotel No 2' and 'A Singer Must Die' and 'Take this Longing' with its unconcealed eroticism and 'Who By Fire' – a dialogue with death.

One sweltering summer night, as we sat in the open window of the flat, looking out over Palmerston Road, dissecting, yet again, the lyrics of one of Leonard's songs, the crusading journalist and women's rights activist Nell McCafferty passed by our garden gate. We called down to her and she waved back and then, appropriately in the circumstances, we returned to the confrontation between the rich and poor and the left and the right and the man and the woman which Leonard sang about in 'There is a War.'

~

Richard and I spent the following couple of summers working in London and there we picked up on Leonard's novels and poetry collections. The discussions were as intense as ever – sometimes about the plays we'd seen in the Royal Court Theatre (we were working just across the road from the theatre, in the kitchens of the

Royal Court Hotel) and, often, about *Beautiful Losers* and *The Favourite Game* – both of which proved disappointing to me. The emotions and experiences I had related to in the songs were absent from the novels and the style of writing didn't appeal to me. The books seemed to lack a narrative drive and the characters at the centre were dull and unrecognisable as real people.

I had come to *Beautiful Losers* with a fascination for one of the characters, the native American saint, Catherine Tekakwitha, but I left the book with a sense that the writing was amphetamine driven and lacked cohesion. I didn't care about the narrators in any of the three sections and only my interest in discovering more about Catherine Tekakwitha kept me reading. Even the sex in the books wasn't particularly exciting!

Again, with his first novel, *The Favourite Game*, I found little I could relate to – the central character, Breavman, didn't hold any great appeal for me and, once I'd finished the book, I didn't have any inclination to reread it.

The worlds of the novels were foreign to me; the characters were not people I'd have wanted to spend time with and the writing seemed to lack any energy or, indeed, to concern itself with things like plot, narrative or even an interest in involving the reader or holding his or her attention. All the things that had attracted me to Leonard's lyric writing seemed not to be there in the novels.

~

His poems were a different matter. Those we both savoured and discussed and read and reread. So many nights in our room in London one or other of us would interrupt the other's reading with: 'Hey, listen to this' or 'what do you think of this for a line?' And when one night a fellow worker tried to burn the house down we fled with our Cohen books under our arms and stood in the street until the police and fire brigade gave the all clear and our workmate was carted off to a psychiatric institution and we returned to our room.

But the songs – even in their absence – were still burning. We didn't have a record player or a cassette deck and the worker downstairs, who did, limited his listening to JJ Cale's *Naturally* and *Really*. Richard and I would throw lines at each other; use them as short-hand when the madness of kitchen-portering got to us. Leonard was the third musketeer on those long summer days.

There were other entertainments in London: free concerts at St Martin in the Fields; plays in marquees in the parks; films that would never be released in Ireland; coming face to face with the magnificence of Van Gogh's *Sunflowers* at the National Gallery; hearing Don Partridge busking in the street outside a cinema on Leicester Square. But Leonard's songs and poems were always at the core of those London summer soundtracks.

~

I went into teaching alive with fire and a commitment to making a mark on my young students' lives. I wanted them to know that education was about more than exams; I wanted them to see that learning opened doors; I wanted them to realise that third-level colleges were not the preserve of the elite, that grants were available, making education more affordable and more important than ever.

In the summer of 1974, I'd been offered three teaching jobs: one in a London convent school; one on a First Nation reservation in Canada and one in my home village of Castledermot. I opted for the home place because I believed I could make a difference there. Within weeks of beginning the job, I'd set up a theatre group for the students; we had a youth club where they could meet and chat and dance on Saturday nights; I started a basketball league on Sunday afternoons. Later, there were trips to Stratford-on-Avon; street theatre; visits to the Abbey Theatre. The world was out there and we were, in our own small way, going out to find it.

In my English and Civics classes I introduced the students to as wide a range of literature and music and political thought as I could and Leonard Cohen's work was a large part of the music I played – along with that of Joan Baez, Pete Seeger, Paul Simon and Judy Collins.

When *Death of a Ladies' Man* arrived, in 1977, it was, again, a radical change of direction. I was familiar with the work of Phil Spector, through the wall of sound groups, and, to my mind, he was hardly the ideal candidate to co-write, or produce, a Leonard Cohen album. Later, Leonard would reveal how, during one of the recording sessions, Spector produced a loaded gun, pointed it at him and said: 'I love you, Leonard.' To which Leonard replied, 'I hope you do, Phil.'

I was already beginning to sail close to the wind in the school, being queried about the topics I was choosing for Civics class debates; asked why I never wore a tie in school (the fact is I didn't and still don't own a tie); questioned about why I had co-written a school play with a student, one of the brightest young men I ever taught. As one of my former pupils said years later, 'You seemed to be hauled into the office more often than we were.'

'True Love Leaves No Traces' was the song that first caught my attention on the *Death of a Ladies Man* and the one I played a hundred times in my room and a dozen times for my students. This was poetry they could understand. Unlike the work of Shakespeare or Hopkins or Yeats, they had an immediate recognition and understanding of the emotion, the experience and the imagery of the lyric.

There were two hills within sight of the school – Rice's Hill which overlooked the village and Mullaghcreelan Hill which rose above the Griese valley. The children from the local National School passed our classroom window every day. When I took the students down to the site of the first monastic settlement in the area, as part of their history and civics studies, we passed along a walkway called The Laurels and, on windy autumn afternoons, the leaves fell on us like tired stars. When we stepped out of the youth club building at midnight, after the disco had ended, we were often looking up at a moonless sky. Everything that was in the lyric of 'True Love Leaves No Traces' was in our village. As with Kavanagh's 'Epic,' the imagery was all around us – the students discerned it in their own lives, even if they hadn't yet found ways of expressing that discernment. They had begun to appreciate and understand that the banal can be poetic and that the poetic and life-changing can be local.

My hope was that this recognition and appreciation would inspire these young women and men to believe in the importance of their own abilities and experiences. More than anything, that was what I wanted for them. I'd been fortunate to have an English teacher in my secondary school who had inspired and encouraged me. Inspiration, as I saw it, was the key concern of my teaching.

I don't know how successful I was in that ambition. Recently I met a man in the cemetery in Castledermot, a former student who had come to visit his wife's grave. He talked about the theatre trips and the music and the school plays and the Saturday night hops and, as he did, his face lit up and, for fifteen minutes, the sadness of the circumstance seemed to leave him and I had a hope that, just perhaps, some small good had been done.

~

Recent Songs was released in 1979 and the work became a staple of my English classes. There were, however, some trades-off. I'd share the songs of Kristofferson, Simon, Brel and Cohen, in return for the occasional Village People, Dr Hook and Pink Floyd track. *The Wall* was hugely popular that year and it opened up significant discussions in Civics classes. That, too, landed me in hot water.

But there were other lessons, too – reminders that music is subjective.

One Friday afternoon, as we wound down for the weekend, a student approached me.

'Are you doing the music at the disco tomorrow night, sir?

'I am.'

'Can I ask a favour, sir?' he asked.

'Sure.'

'You won't bring your Leonard Cohen records, will you?'

'No,' I promised, 'I won't.'

'Thanks, sir. They're grand in class but they're not great for dances.'

He blushed but I understood.

~

Recent Songs is among my favourite Leonard Cohen collections. The opening track, 'The Guests' is one of his most beautiful, soulful, reassuring and mystical creations. (Forty years later, I would use lines from the song on the programme cover of a requiem Mass I would write with Leonard.) The juxtaposition of the open-hearted many and the broken-hearted few, with the open-hearted few and the broken-hearted many, bookends an enigmatic song that reeks of life, death, hope and despair. It's a lyric that delicately interlaces faith and futility.

For me, the song held reverberations of my mother's relatively recent death but it also carried that amalgam of ghost story; love story and the confusion that is, so often, the human condition. I was twenty-six when the album was released, my health was good and I was busy and fit but I was, too, aware of mortality. Death seemed, suddenly, to have taken a liking to our school.

A number of young people from the classes I'd taught – most quite recently graduated – had died in tragic circumstances: some in motor cycle accidents; one in a car crash; one in childbirth; one in the week of her marriage. As 'The Guests' says, no one knows the where, when, how or why of those moments where living becomes dying and dying becomes death.

The young women and men who died had entered death in *every style of passion*. But, truth be told, I was as earnestly lost, in my own way, as they were in theirs. The dream of changing lives was being ground out of me by a system that was, more and more, about the academic and, less and less, about the vocational.

The implementation of a new schooling plan in the village which would see the local Secondary school coalesce with the Vocational school into a Community school where the emphasis would be on the academic side of education just didn't appeal to me. Examinations were not the reason I'd come into teaching and so I began to consider other career paths.

Meanwhile, I was still playing the music in my classes. The tone set by 'The Guests' paved the way for the other gems on *Recent Songs,* superb lyrics and tunes on a collection that is blessed with a particular grace and tenderness. Among them is the extraordinary 'Our Lady of Solitude.'

If ever Leonard melded the sacred and the sensual, he has done it in this song. To hear those opening words sung was, for me, to be drawn into a world that absolutely mirrored my own. The carnality of the opening verse is immediate and I recognised that – the object of his affection is there and all summer long she has touched him. Nothing could be clearer or more sexual. And yet, as the song progresses, it becomes clear that this isn't simply an erotic relationship – the images that appear are perfumed, scented with the sacred, too. The light from the woman's body; the dress of silver and blue; the very title of the song paralleled the carnal with the sanctified. This was familiar territory to me – a woman as the mother of God and a woman as Eve. This was the terrain I'd grown up hearing about from the pulpit and in the confession box and on school retreats. But here Leonard was presenting both facets of the female, not just in one song but in one woman. That was something new and electrifying.

~

Recent Songs closes with 'Ballad of the Absent Mare.'

There are three songs, ostensibly about horses, that have long intrigued me. The first is the Byrds 'Chestnut Mare' which captivated me from the moment I first bought the vinyl double-album *The Best of the Byrds: Greatest Hit Volume II*. Like Leonard's track, that song tells the story of the chase and the escape – the writer/rider captures the mare but she escapes in the end and he's left with the ambition of catching her, again, one day. It may well be that the mare is a metaphorical drug trip but it's also true that the song was partly inspired by a story in Ibsen's *Peer Gynt*, a story about a boy chasing a reindeer and taking a magical flight on the animal's back.

The second horse song that I love is Ian Anderson's 'Heavy Horses' from Jethro Tull's 1978 album of the same name. When I interviewed Ian Anderson in the eighties, he said the song was inspired by the heavy horses which had been so much a part of farm life around his estate in Buckinghamshire but which were, by then, consigned to being show animals. And, of course, the band's name, also the name of an eighteenth century English agronomist, brought the connection with the land and agriculture full circle.

The third horse-inspired song that has long enthralled me is Leonard's 'Ballad of the Absent Mare.' Like 'Chestnut Mare,' this song has a literary inspiration, although I didn't realise that when first I heard it. What did catch my attention was the yearning in the lyric and the beauty of the language.

Later, I would learn that the song has its roots in Zen teaching but that information was still several years down the line for me and would come, when it did, from the writer's mouth.

~

Leonard toured Europe again in 1980 but the tour didn't include Ireland. By chance, that was the year I stepped away from my job as a teacher of English and History. I left Castledermot Vocational School that summer without telling the students I wouldn't be back. It's a decision I still regret and one I've struggled to explain to myself. I think I felt guilty – that I was leaving them; that I was, as I saw it, abandoning a dream of making a difference. But I think, too, I was already burnt out. Over the six years of teaching I had committed myself to the classroom and the extra-curricular as well as my personal life, politics, involvement in a theatre company and in writing.

I had come to the realisation that the system wasn't going to be beaten and so I left.

~

The previous year I had been involved in Community Radio, run by RTE, and the producer, Paddy O'Neill, suggested I apply for a job in RTE. I did and my initial application was unsuccessful but I applied again and landed a job on 2FM, producing an education programme presented by an up and coming broadcaster called Gerry Ryan.

That career change would bring me into contact with Leonard for the first time.

Four

In 1984 Leonard released *Various Positions* or, more accurately, the album escaped. It slipped into shops and made hardly a ripple, sales wise. That was something I found extraordinary. The album contained three songs that were to become staples not only of Leonard's set-list but of those of many other singers: 'Dance Me to the End of Love;' 'Hallelujah' and 'If It Be Your Will.'

Leonard described the writing and recording of the songs on the album as 'almost painfully joyful' but it was on the back of the finished record that Sony President Walter Yetnikoff famously remarked: 'Look, Leonard, we know you're a genius, we just don't know if you're any good.'

~

'If It Be Your Will' is a song about the Holocaust but, for me, it brings back memories of a smaller, more intimate tragedy. On a Sunday afternoon in late 1984 I was driving home from Dublin to Athy on a clear, straight, four-lane road. I had a copy of *Various Positions* in the cassette player of the car. I had finished work in RTE about an hour earlier and was looking forward to the basketball match I would play later in the afternoon.

As I drove, I noticed two cars on the opposite carriageway. One slowed to turn left and the car behind bumped it as it turned. There was minimal contact and I still don't know why I stopped but I did. With little traffic in either direction, I crossed the road to where the two cars were now stationary. I could see that neither car had sustained any significant damage but neither the driver nor his female companion had got out of the first car.

I opened their passenger door and the woman handed me a baby who had obviously been in her arms.

'Are you ok?' I asked.

The woman gestured toward the infant I was now holding.

'I think she's dead,' she said quietly. And she was. Despite the mildness of the jolt, the baby's head had come into contact with the dashboard.

Years later, I'd remember that incident when I'd hear another brutal story about a baby from Zoltan Zinn Collis who was a survivor of the Holocaust. But, on that bright Sunday afternoon, I stood holding the infant, dressed in her rags of light, while the middle-aged man who had been driving the second car sat, grey-faced on the roadside and the baby's parents remained in silence in their car, unable to move.

Extraordinarily, 'Hallelujah' passed most people by on its release, its genius unrecognised. Yet there are so many strands of wonder in that song. As with Isaac and Joan of Arc, Leonard took a figure from history and put flesh on his bones and explored the appetite that would be his downfall.

The David in the Old Testament who fascinated me was not the king but the man on the roof spying on the naked Bathsheba as she bathed in the river. Driven by his lust for her, nothing would stand in his way. But it wasn't simply her naked body that drew David to her – it was something more than that, it was her beauty and the moonlight that created the moment. That detail (like Paul Simon's line in 'America' about the moon rising *over an open field*) creates a breath-taking moment when you hear it. And the way in which the song slides into the Samson story (the cutting of the hair) but setting it in the domesticity of any house in any town (when he's tied to a kitchen chair) is another mark of genuinely extraordinary writing. I'd always thought, on hearing the story read in church, that, much more than the supposed events in the Garden of Eden, the tale of David and Bathsheba was relatable to human disorder and to the tempting attractions of circumstance, place and person.

Over the years I've heard so many singers misread the lyric of the third verse – singing about learning *to shoot somebody* when, in fact, the lyric is *to shoot at somebody*. If, as the song says, the other guy *outdrew you* then the shooting *at* throws a whole new light on the situation and its meaning.

In the second last verse Leonard, again, brings together, immaculately, the sexual and the spiritual. His vision of the sexual act as one of mysticism and inspiration suddenly blows away all the decades of Church teaching on sex as sin.

The closing verse, where Leonard speaks about being unable to feel but trying to touch instead, is an image that has followed me all my life, reflecting my own experience of the struggle to be intimate and open with others and, as a result, often choosing to confuse physical contact with emotional connection.

'Hallelujah' holds so much more than it is given credit for.

~

The following year, 1985, Leonard and his band returned to Ireland for two concerts. By then, I was working as a producer with RTE Radio 2 which, as it happened, was the worst and the best of things. Because of work commitments, I didn't get to either of those concerts but, as producer of a programme called *Favourite Five* – a version of Desert Island Discs – presented by the exceptional Ken Stewart, I did get to meet Leonard for the first time.

I clearly remember phoning Sony records in New York to arrange the interview for that programme; the conversation is still fresh in my mind almost forty years later. The publicity person to whom I spoke seemed puzzled by my call.

'I'm sorry,' she said, 'I have no idea who you're talking about?'

'Leonard Cohen. He's one of your artists and he's touring Europe and I wanted to set up an interview while he's in Dublin.'

'I think you're mistaken,' she said. 'We don't have a Leonard Cohen on our label.'

'His latest album was released just last year. It's called *Various Positions*.'

'I'm sorry, sir, but there is no such album on our catalogue. And there's no such artist.'

'Suzanne;' 'So Long Marianne;' 'Bird on the Wire'...do those songs ring a bell?'

'Vaguely, sir, but your Mr...ehm...Cohen is absolutely not an artist on our label. I'm sorry I can't be of any further help. Have a nice day.'

Executives at Sony records in the United States had decided there was no point in releasing the record there at all. The publicist was right; it wasn't on their catalogue because it had been ditched.

Despite that setback, through the good offices of the promoter, an interview was arranged.

~

The *Favourite Five* programme was recorded in Leonard's bedroom in Jury's Hotel in Ballsbridge in Dublin on the morning after the second show. Ken Stewart sat on one bed, Leonard sat on the other and, appropriately, given their respective standings as a presenter with an encyclopaedic knowledge of popular music and a genius of creativity, I knelt between them holding the mic and keeping an eye on the fifteen minute reel-to-reel tape in the Uher tape recorder.

The five songs chosen by Leonard were: 'Take These Chains from My Heart' (Ray Charles); 'Tangled Up in Blue (Bob Dylan); 'Jezebel' (Frankie Laine); 'Piece of my Heart (Janis Joplin) and a Rodrigo's 'Andante' (John Williams).

Ken's interview threw up several insights into Leonard's life. Asked whether he had a large record collection, he talked about the difficulty of carrying records from place to place. 'I buy cassettes but keep leaving them around,' he said.

And the first record he bought? 'I bought the first LP that was issued in Canada; we had 78s up to that. The first LP I bought was *Annie Get Your Gun*…I didn't like it so much but I was just interested in the technology.'

He talked about the musical influences in his house as a young boy, referencing his father who loved the music of Gilbert and Sullivan and the Scottish singer and comedian, Harry Lauder.

When Ken raised the subject of country music, Leonard was heartfelt in his response: 'I always loved country music, I grew up with country music and I still like to play it…It's very much underestimated by intellectual critics. It's a real people's music.'

In that sentence lay the kernel of Leonard's approach to music and to life. He was a highly intelligent man with a brilliant intellect, yet he disliked the intellectual snobbery that surrounded so much of music and literature. The people were important to him because he was one of the people. That never drew him into lowering his literary or musical standards because he had an innate confidence in the intelligence of the reader and listener to understand and accompany his characters on their journeys. He trusted the reader and he trusted the listener.

In that interview with Ken Stewart, Leonard spoke about his guitar playing and referenced a Spanish guitarist he met when he was fifteen. Decades later, in his acceptance speech at the Prince of Asturias Award in 2011, he would speak again about the young guitarist who taught him the chords he would use in his music and revealed that the young man had taken his own life in Canada. Leonard went on to talk about his economical style of guitar playing and added: 'I know my voice is very limited and I'm just drawn to economical expression.'

Ken then asked him about Yeats' reference to seizing the moments between ripe and rotten. Leonard responded: 'If you operate on a level of fifty percent success you're doing pretty well. I think that's about all you can hope for. You know, you get older and realise there are consequences to your mistakes. That's the only thing you get with old age, it doesn't mean you avoid the mistakes, it just means you've got to pay for them.'

The interview ended with a left-field question about what Leonard might put on his own tombstone. There was a hiatus before he said: 'You'd have to give me a moment to come up with......' and his voice trailed off.

As it happens, the words on his headstone couldn't be simpler. Under the image of the unified hearts, which he designed, are his name, LEONARD COHEN, and then the dates, 1934 – 2016. The rest can be found in the writing.

The interview over, I packed up the tapes and recorder and then produced, from a brown paper bag, Leonard's two novels, a couple of his poetry collections and copies of his records to date.

'I wonder if you'd mind signing these,' I asked

'I'd be happy to, man.'

That done, I had one final favour to ask.

'Would you mind if we had a photograph with you. My daughter, Lydia, is outside.'

'Of course not,' he said. 'Bring her in.'

Lydia was almost four at the time and Ken Stewart took the photograph.

'I have to find some candy for your daughter,' Leonard said, opening his packed suitcase and rooting about inside but no candy could be found. Instead, he took a flower from the bouquet on the bedroom table and presented it to her and then, as though his time and generosity were not already enough, he unpinned a guitar brooch from his jacket and gave that to her, too.

And so the first meeting ended. We headed back to the radio centre to edit the tapes and Leonard headed for the airport and a flight to Brussels. I presumed that would be my first and last contact with him.

Five

One of the things I regularly did on Friday afternoons in the eighties was to swing by Sony records in Dublin to see whether there was anything new on release, any music that might be of interest for the programmes I was producing on RTE.

On a bitter afternoon before Christmas 1986 one of the albums I was given was *Famous Blue Raincoat* by Jennifer Warnes, a collection of eight Cohen covers and two new songs: 'First We Take Manhattan,' a Leonard song, and 'Song of Bernadette,' co-written by Jennifer Warnes, Bill Elliott and Leonard. Anything new from Leonard's pen was of immediate interest.

Coincidentally, at the time of the album's release, I had been toying with the idea of writing a mockumentary for radio on the life of Bernadette Soubirous, the Bernadette of Lourdes and part subject of the Jennifer Warnes' song. I wanted to create a dramatization of Bernadette Soubirous' life but in documentary form, including *interviews* with Bernadette and her contemporaries – based on the transcriptions made at the many questionings she had undergone following the reported apparitions at Lourdes. The song seemed like an encouragement in that direction. (The programme would get made some time later.)

In an interview about the song, Jennifer Warnes referred to the fact that her given name was Bernadette but her siblings preferred the name Jennifer and so, a week after her birth, the family opted for Jennifer. She talked about the duality of carrying both names, one of a saint and one, as she put it, of a woman 'who had fallen for the world.' In a commentary, on the Franciscan Sisters website, she spoke about how that contrast of names and ways of dealing with the world led her to write a series of letters between Jennifer and Bernadette. She said the letters were an experiment, saying things like: *Dear Bernadette, I'm so lost right now*. And replying: *Hello dear Jennifer, don't worry, I'm here and it's going to be okay*. The kind of conversation many of us have with ourselves.

She showed the letters to Leonard and he said: 'There's a song in there. Just start at the beginning. "There was a child named Bernadette, I heard the story long ago..." and then keep going.'

The release of *Famous Blue Raincoat* and the faith Jennifer Warnes had in Leonard's work suddenly brought his songs to a new and wider audience. His one-time backing singer was carrying a much needed banner for Leonard's flagging career, reminding people of just how brilliant a songwriter he really was.

~

On another Friday afternoon, a spring evening in 1988, I collected some singles and albums from Sony, among them was the new Leonard Cohen release – *I'm Your Man*. Apart from the LP, I was given a cassette copy and it went into the cassette player in the car the moment I hit the road.

Where *Recent Songs* had been deeply introspective in music and words, *I'm Your Man* was something entirely different. The sound – with Leonard on keyboard – and the production were something new for him and, certainly, for me. From the opening track, 'First We Take Manhattan' there was a distinctive and powerful and innovative attitude. But it was a pair of tracks on side two that caught and held my attention. 'Take This Waltz,' adapted from a poem by Leonard's long-time poetic hero, Federico Garcia Lorca, mesmerised me. (Leonard once said, 'Lorca is one of those rare poets with whom you can stay in love for life.')

The imagery of Lorca's poem, 'Pequeno Vals Vienés,' is surreal yet real. The images and impressions tumble from the poem and from the song. One moment it's a perplexity, the next a flash of enlightening clarity. The song, it seems to me, has a more intense sensuality and eroticism than the poem. Partly that's down to the voice, partly to the music, but mostly it's down to the way in which Leonard has taken Lorca's images and woven them into something more tangible and more experiential than the poem appears to do.

Leonard has stayed true to the spirit of the original but has melded these curious images with heartening music to create a work of real energy, passion and sensuality.

What is it that draws me to one song over another? Mostly it's the lyric – though I do have a tendency to prefer slower songs. But, at the heart of the songs I love is the one key element of connection. There's always something with which I can associate – an idea; an experience; a phrase; an image that is recognisable. Those are the links that pull me in.

Just as 'True Love Leaves No Traces' had rung bells for me in the context of my home village, 'Take This Waltz' – and particularly the closing verse – reminded me of the beauty of south Kildare and the landscape that had so inspired my writing: Mullaghcreelan Wood and the valley below it; the cornfields and hedgerows around Castledermot; the roadside ditches splashed with colour from early spring to late autumn. Again, the song and the poem, had performed that elegiac miracle of making the universal local.

A few years later, I adapted four lines from the poem/song for my own headstone, though, partly because I've never been much of a dancer, I've since opted for an entirely different quote from Leonard to be that epitaph.

My version of the Lorca/Cohen lines read:

I'll dance with you among lilacs,
I'll be wearing a forest's disguise;
the red poppy wild on your shoulder,
in cornflowers the blue of your eyes.

~

The other song on *I'm Your Man* that went straight onto rewind and repeat was 'Tower of Song.' An homage to, among other things, country music; it's filled with gently desolate portraits, wry humour (something that so many critics missed over the years when they dismissed Leonard's work as 'razor blade music') and an astonishing take on bitterness and his personal experience of overcoming it.

The lines about the figure standing on the other side and his not knowing how the river got so wide are a universal reality captured in seventeen words. Whether it's an absent love; a broken friendship or a loss through death, the imprint of that distant, unreachable figure about which Leonard writes has never left me. Over the years, the identity of the figure has changed; sometimes it's a friend; sometimes a neighbour; sometimes my mother, my father, my brother but the vision is still the same. And, though those bridges to engagement have been irreparably destroyed, I still identify with the feeling of aching nearness to every cherished soul who has vanished and there's some consolation in that response.

Allied to all of this, the song holds Leonard's promise, which has proven so true, that we'd be hearing from him long after he'd gone.

Six

In June 1988, Leonard came to Dublin for two shows in the National Stadium, on Saturday June 4. I caught the second of those concerts and the set list included the established ('Bird on the Wire;' 'Sisters of Mercy;' 'The Partisan' and 'Suzanne') and the more recent, including, to my delight, 'Take This Waltz.' The show finished with a stunning version of 'Whither Thou Goest.' In the silences between the acapella lines, you could hear a tear drop in the stadium. Yet again, Leonard had done something unforeseen and, in my case, sent me out into the night with a new take on the Old Testament story of Ruth and Naomi.

More exciting for me, however, than the concert, was the fact that I got the opportunity to interview Leonard for the first time. Again, the venue was Jury's Hotel, this time in a downstairs room which had been set aside for a morning of meetings with journalists.

I explained to Leonard that what I had in mind was to make two programmes based around his work – one on the figures who appeared in his songs, from Isaac to Joan of Arc, and one about truth, love and loss in the songs.

His response was positive. 'Let's do it, man.'

~

We began our discussion with 'Story of Isaac,' that brilliant retelling of an old story.

'I was careful in that song to try to put it beyond the simple anti-war protest that it also is. It says at the end there, "the man of war, the man of peace, the peacock spreads his deadly fan."

'In other words, it isn't necessarily for war that we're willing to sacrifice each other. We'll get some idea – some magnificent idea – that we're willing to sacrifice each other for; it doesn't necessarily have to involve an opponent or an ideology, but human beings, being what they are, we're always going to set up people to die for some absurd situation that we define as important.'

He went on to talk about the lure of the persuasive: 'I'm very suspicious of charismatic holy men and compelling oratories and, yes, shining statesmen – very suspicious – but I mean my heart goes out to them, too, because if I didn't recognise my own vulnerability to that charm I wouldn't be talking about it at all.'

Staying with the Old Testament, we discussed 'Hallelujah' and the characters that people that song. I remember clearly that Leonard warmed to the subject as he spoke, leaning in across the table, gently moving a coffee cup to one side.

'Finally, there's no conflict between things,' he said. 'Finally, everything is reconciled but not where we live. This world is full of conflicts and full of things that cannot be reconciled but there are moments where we can transcend the dualistic system, and reconcile and embrace the whole mess, and that's what I mean by Hallelujah. That regardless of what the impossibility of the situation is; there is a moment when you open your mouth and you throw open your arms and you embrace the thing and you just say "Hallelujah! Blessed is the name." And you can't reconcile it in any other way except in that position of total surrender, total affirmation.'

Our inability to change things, our having to accept things and, yet, celebrating that powerlessness is at the centre of 'Hallelujah.'

'That's what it's all about. It says that none of this – you're not going to be able to work this thing out – this realm does not admit to resolution – there's no solution to this mess. The only moment that you can live here comfortably in these absolutely irreconcilable conflicts is in this moment when you embrace it all and say: "Look, I don't understand a fucking thing at all – Hallelujah!" That's the only moment that we live here fully as human beings.'

The conversation veered off to a brief chat about 'Passing Through,' the Richard Blakeslee song, written in 1948 and recorded by, among others, Pete Seeger. Leonard had recorded it on his *Live Songs* album. I wondered what had drawn him to the song, with its parade of characters from history: Jesus on the cross, talking of love not hate; Adam leaving the garden, praying for rain, planning to raise a little Cain/cane; George Washington at the Valley Forge vowing that men will fight – and die – for what is right, and Franklin D Roosevelt promising that one world will come out of World War Two?

'I like to hear anybody's story,' Leonard told me. 'The people whose stories I like to hear are, you know, people who have gone right down the line for it in some way.'

Returning to Leonard's own compositions, we talked about 'Chelsea Hotel.' I put it to him that the notion of people suffering for their art can sometimes seem artificial and precious to those who make their livings as factory workers or shop assistants. Again, he became animated: 'I don't think anybody beats the rap in this world. You know, I mean there are people far more powerful, far more successful than me, you know that as a human being living life on the front line of your own life, as everybody lives their life, there's no free ride, everybody understands that. Everybody understands that every single thing you get you pay for, especially things like love, especially things like artistic success. There's nobody who beats the rap in this game,'

I suggested that while he talks about the oppression of beauty, it's what most of us are looking for in art and music and life – beauty.

'I think there are people who make their work beautiful in a way they can never make their lives or their bodies beautiful,' Leonard said. 'I mean, I know Janis Joplin, I mean she was the classic pop star, as embodied by the rose in that movie. She really would sing to twenty- or thirty-thousand people who were drooling at her feet and, you know, I'd see her wandering around the Chelsea Hotel at three in the morning trying to find, you know, someone to have a cup of coffee with. So, how do you reconcile those things? I don't know. She stood for something beautiful and nervous and high and surrendered completely and yet she couldn't have those things, she couldn't manifest those things, simple beautiful things in her life, that's really what I mean.'

The pervading feeling in Chelsea Hotel is one of uncertainty. There's no question of love, just what's called love. Then there's the anti-romantic closing, about not being able to keep track of each fallen robin. A line redolent of Matthew's Gospel, verse 10, where Jesus says not one sparrow will fall outside his Father's care.

We moved in the interview from Janis Joplin to Bernadette Soubirous and the song he had co-written with Jennifer Warnes and Bill Elliott. Though not a song he had recorded, I was fascinated by his thoughts on the work and his contribution to it.

'Jennifer was brought up as a Catholic girl and we were on tour together and she was talking about Bernadette all the time and I always was fascinated by the figure, too, and she said I really want you to write me a song about Bernadette, here's like a couple of lines of a tune, here's my idea. So the song came out, it was a real collaboration; we really worked together on the thing.'

I remarked that I thought 'Song of Bernadette' works on several levels. There's the young visionary of February and March 1858 with that apparition in her soul, a vision in which no one else believed. And, there are the rest of us with our own visions and dreams, in which no one, least of all ourselves, can truly believe. Once we come to a moment of realisation that visions don't last, we end up running and falling, rather than flying. Bernadette is true to her belief and is finally rewarded with the knowledge that there is mercy in the world. But the song also acknowledges that each of us is torn by what we've done and can't undo.

Leonard nodded in agreement, 'I think that we mostly do fail in these things, but the thing that makes these failures supportable are these moments, like the one I tried to talk about in 'Hallelujah' or the one I tried to talk about in Bernadette, it's those are the moments when the thing is resolved – the thing is reconciled – not actually by moving pieces around. It's not a chess game. As I say in my new version of 'Hallelujah,' "I've seen your flag on the marble arch, but love is not a victory march, it's a cold and it's a broken Hallelujah." Nobody's going to win this, not the men, not the women, not the socialists, not the conservatives. Nobody's going to win this deal. The only time we win is that moment when we drop the battle and we affirm the whole situation with this embrace.'

Ultimately, 'Song of Bernadette' is a plea for love. It's a celebration of hope and faith; a statement of belief that we can get through to something clearer. It's one of Cohen's fiercest and most powerful lyrics.

There was a moment of silence, a moment of contemplation and then Leonard added: 'But I never sang the song alone; I've only sung it with Jennifer. It's a beautiful song I think.'

I had a question on the tip of my tongue but, foolishly, I left it unasked for then and, when I finally got around to asking it, fate intervened and the moment was lost.

~

The most enigmatic, most energetic, most exciting of the heroines in Leonard's songs is a compatriot of Bernadette Soubirous. Joan of Arc was a soldier and a mould breaker. She, too, was a girl adrift in a political world she didn't fully understand or embrace. 'Joan of Arc' concentrates on the human being, the uncertain one behind the armour. Leonard views her as a woman pursued by fire until eventually, inevitably, that fire is her consuming passion.

In the song, Joan is alone in her tent, the army dependent on her clarity of mind; a nation tied to her strategy. And what we find in that tent is a woman without interest in the war. Her armour is no longer bright; she is without a man to get her through the night. She craves a wedding dress, something white, and something at odds with the fighting about her. So, is Leonard Cohen saying a woman ultimately needs a man to be fulfilled? Not quite!

'I was thinking more of this sense of a destiny that human beings have and how they meet and marry their destiny, how ultimately there is, you know, a male or a minus-plus, however you want to put it, you know, a positive-negative, yin-yang, male-female; that there is this connection that we have with our – with the unfolding of our lives. I don't want to suggest in that song that what she really wanted to be was a housewife. What I mean to say is that as lonely and as solitudinous as she was, she had to meet and be embraced by her destiny. That's all I mean by that imagery. I've just been reading a lot about Joan of Arc again, she continues to fascinate me, that woman, and seen from the point of view of the woman's movement she really does stand for something stunningly original and courageous. There's a great chapter about her in Andrea Dworkin's book, *Intercourse*. It's a grand chapter on Joan of Arc and really a passionate evocation of what her real achievement was at the time, to by-pass everything and to go right into the centre of activity. So I don't mean to suggest that she really wanted a wedding ring and some kids and day-care.'

In the end, it's the woman and the passion that remain: Joan and the fire. She can climb inside that fire, not in defeat, but believing in its glory – to a personal, sexual and spiritual fulfilment. It no longer matters what people think. Perhaps she is Joan of Arc; perhaps she's just a piece of wood. Perhaps she initially winces in pain, but after the tears there's the glory – the long sought love and light. And what's true for Joan is true for all of us. Love and light, once found, must be taken. They come with cruelty, they dazzle and hurt. But, for the here and now, they're all we have.

Seven

The second programme I made with Leonard was titled, *If I Have Been Untrue*. In it, we explored the songs he had written about the human condition, not as it affected the heroic figures of history but how we live our lives, do our jobs, fall in and out of love, betray and are betrayed.

That programme began with his live version of 'Please Don't Pass Me By' but the song I chose to discuss first was 'Bird on the Wire,' the song with which, for years, he had opened his concerts. A song as powerful in its understatement as 'Please Don't Pass Me By' is in its overstatement. 'Bird on the Wire' is a song of darkness, but it had its genesis in the light of Greece.

'I think it was just reportage,' Leonard said. 'I remember sitting beside a window in my house in Greece years ago and I think they just put up the telephone wires. There hadn't been any telephone wires or electric wires and no electricity, and I just noticed the bird on the wire there. And the next image comes from there – from that little village, too, where I used to live – where other late night drinkers would come home, you know, maybe two, three in the morning, and they'd stumble through the streets with their arms around each other's shoulders singing these, you know, just perfect three part harmonies. And nobody ever minded because even if you woke up to those strains you didn't mind.

I put it to Leonard that the imagery of 'Bird on the Wire' begins with attempted freedom - the bird and the drunk in the midnight choir – and moves to captivity – a hooked worm, a knight trapped in a book – and finally goes deeper, to pain, with the poignant image of a still born baby tearing those who have reached out for its birth and its life. I was thinking of my own parents and their stillborn children.

The song eventually synthesises in Cohen's long held belief that there is no perfection in this world, and his appeal for any unkindness he may be guilty of to be forgiven. He insists that he has never really been untrue, not in his soul. There are echoes of Ernest Dowson's 'Cynara' – 'I have been faithful to thee, Cynara, in my fashion.' The figures offering advice are a beggar and a woman in a darkened door. The beggar urges Cohen not to ask so much of life, the woman urges that he ask for more. In the face of it all Cohen keeps faith with love – it's the best that can be done.

'I think whatever that means to us when we hear that expression 'keeping the faith', I think that's…you know a lot of people live and die by that.'

In spite of keeping faith, it seems to me that there is, too, in this complex song, the assertion that love inevitably causes as much pain as pleasure.

'Whenever you really walk into that, which only happens now and then I guess – well it happens with your kids, it happens with your parents, it happens with your mate. If you ever surrender the self, if you ever let the self die for a moment, then of course you're going to experience suffering, you're going to know what it's about. Because to surrender means you have to stop maintaining this hero at the centre of your own drama. Yet we spend most of our energy maintaining this hero. And this hero is doomed because nobody can live at the centre of the drama thinking that he's the hero and that everybody else has some kind of lesser role. So that's precisely the character we have to surrender when we move into that field of love, and it's always painful for him to take off his armour. He gets wounded immediately because there are arrows flying all over the place. As soon as he takes off his hero's costume he goes down with an arrow in his heart, that's why, you know, the figure of Cupid arose. You go down with that arrow in your heart, it's no joke. It's no joke. You feel it with your children, you feel it with your mate, and you feel it with your parents, you feel it with your friends. If ever you take off the hero's armour, you get hit right away.'

I talked, briefly, to Leonard about the circumstances of my first hearing his work and of how, in that near-death condition, Anna Marly and Hy Zaret's song, 'The Partisan,' had rung so true and how Leonard had filled the song with an extraordinary feeling, as though he were singing from experience, as though he were the partisan.

'Well there's something of course, there's something always attractive about that kind of figure. But deeper than that there's something that's always attracted me about the notion of a resistance, and sometimes that feeling gets – it's a subtle feeling – sometimes it's very clear there are things it's worthwhile calling people on. But as the scene gets more and more complex it becomes clear to me that there is a kind of resistance and all of us are on both sides or participate on the many sides of this complexity. But somewhere there's something in everybody that says: Well, the public life doesn't represent me. And the public statements don't represent me, and my life is not represented on television. My life is not represented in the politician's plans. My life is not represented in the books and the songs. That there's something, that there's a big gap between my private life and the public expression. And I think we're in one of those times now. That gap opens and closes.'

'The Partisan' can be read in two ways: the central figure resisting the imposition of ideas, and also the specific resistance of the French Underground to the German occupation during the Second World

War. The French version of the song is clear on this: 'The Germans were in my home. They told me to resign myself, but I'm not afraid', and later, 'an old man kept us for the night in an attic. The Germans took him - he's dead. I've lost my wife and children but I've many friends. I have all of France.' One can easily imagine Leonard being drawn to that figure.

'That figure, the protagonist of that song is really actively engaged in the war against fascism or tyranny or oppression. It's a little more complex right now because in a certain sense things have never been better. That's when it really becomes diabolic, is when things have never been better and you just know that there's this little numb part of your heart that is not being addressed by anything. That's when the soul becomes deeply threatened.'

Our conversation moved to a figure closer to Leonard's own life – Nancy Challies – who took her life at the age of twenty-one, after her daughter had been put up for adoption. Leonard admitted that 'at least the genesis of the song is connected with a young woman in Montreal…I think that the world throws up certain kinds of figures. Sometime in abundance, sometimes very rarely, and that some of these figures act as archetypes or prototypes for another generation which will manifest these characteristics a lot more easily, maybe a lot more gracefully, but not a lot more heroically. Because I think that these prototypes, that are thrown up in the generation before they manifest in abundance, are always very interesting and heroic figures, and Nancy I feel was one of those figures, maybe a sixties figure or a nineties figure, that was somehow manifested in the fifties.'

Finally, Nancy is isolated; unable, despite her strength, to exist in a vacuum. Using her brother's gun, she takes her own life. What, I wondered, was so attractive about Nancy? Her heroism? Her vulnerability? Or both?

'It's something like – it's something beyond choice. You know it's something...she just took things out of the air and acted on them without any regard to their consequence because she didn't have a choice in the matter. Another twenty years later she would have been just like, you know, the hippest girl on the block. But twenty years before she was...there was no reference to her, so in a certain way she was doomed. If a person doesn't have any reference in their lives and nobody can place them anywhere, they're in grave danger. They don't have any support themselves.'

And then Leonard paused for a long time before singing, very quietly, as though he had forgotten I was there, 'It seems so long ago...'

I waited a moment and he made eye contact, smiled and we continued our conversation, moving on to a track from *Recent Songs*, 'Our Lady of Solitude.'

Like the earlier 'Sisters of Mercy,' the title of this has a strongly religious feel, a feeling Leonard doesn't deny. But there's more to the song. It reflects a Christian influence but goes further, into pantheism, though, ultimately, it seems to me, that the imagery is strongly Catholic: the light from the lady's body, her dress of blue and silver, the fact that she is the vessel of the world – reflective of Mary's title as Vessel of Honour, Devotion and Mystical Rose in Catholic prayer.

'Well I don't think you can ignore those associations and I come from a very Catholic city myself and those images - you see I have a very sympathetic take of Catholicism and Christianity because I wasn't brought up as a Christian or a Catholic, but I saw it operating from the outside, so to speak, and I didn't have to suffer any of the things that my friends say they suffered from it, although they seemed to be pretty healthy and pretty tough and pretty soulful people. Even the ones who complain about the tyranny of their Catholic education - I always said to myself, well I'm sure they're complaining about something that is real but they seem to turn out pretty good, in spite of it. So maybe there is a certain genius to that education that operates even though, you know, there's an occasional thorn and a stick. But anyways - no you can't disassociate the Catholic imagery from that song, I mean that is the virgin of the world, but even the church can't conceal that these things have deeper origins and refer to even more ancient mysteries.'

And more sensual, I suggested. In the song, Leonard thanks the lady for keeping him close while so many others stood apart. So, I wondered, would he term himself religious?

'Well I would never claim that title for myself, I mean not

remotely. But I do feel certain connections with certain entities or forces.'

Pursuing that point, I asked about his most recent publication, *Book of Mercy*, a deeply spiritual work.

'Well I guess, you know, I think that everybody leads a spiritual life. I don't know if it's even worthwhile to designate it as that way. Everybody is in touch with their own resources, with their own deep pools of divine activity, otherwise they wouldn't be here on this plane - they'd evaporate. I mean everybody is living a so-called religious life, everybody lives a so-called spiritual life, everybody is in touch with these powers otherwise they wouldn't be around.'

So, did he see spirituality, rather than organised religion, as the answer to a lot of problems?

'I don't want ever to set myself up as an enemy of organised religion because those churches, those mosque, those synagogues, they give comfort and solace to millions and millions of people, and real comfort and real solace, so I don't think it serves anything or anybody to become an enemy of organised religion. Organised religion, on the inside is very tender to its members. On the outside, it tends to be antagonistic to the other organised religions. They tend on the inside to act like family, on the outside they tend to act like states, and they're continually putting themselves in an abrasive position in regard to one another. That, I think, is deeply sinful.'

All of those ideas are hinted at in 'Our Lady of Solitude.' She gathered in his soul. She touched him. Her fingers were the fingers of a weaver. There was light from her body. Her words were few and small. She was the mistress of us all. Perhaps she was the woman who appeared to Bernadette Soubirous, perhaps the encapsulation of womanhood.

The conversation moved from the spiritual to the political and the song 'A Singer Must Die,' a song I'd always reckoned to be one of Leonard's most overtly political songs, though I wouldn't have classed the bulk of his other songs as political. He disagreed.

'I think all my songs are political in a certain way, but that one especially in the recorded version where the last verse is really very strong against a certain kind of authority.'

I mention the fact that I sometimes feel I'm listening to the ghost of Victor Jara when I hear that song and I wonder where it came from?

'I guess that's some kind of basic view I hold about the thing,' Leonard says, ' that it doesn't really matter what the singer is speaking of, it doesn't really matter what the song is. There's something I listen for in a singer's voice and that's some kind of truth. It may even be the truth of deception, it may even be the truth of the scam, the truth of the hustle in the singer's own presentation, but something is coming across that is true, and if that isn't there the song dies. And the singer deserves to die too, and will, in time, die. So the thing that I listen for is that note, is that note of something big manifested that is beyond the singer's control.'

‘A Singer Must Die’ was significantly rewritten, moving it out of the specifically political realm and widening its relevance. Making the issues more mundane and, thus, more universal. Bringing the war down to a struggle between individuals, Leonard talks about being saved a place in the ten dollar grave with those who took money for the pleasure they gave, with those who undressed so any of us could lie down with our heads on their breasts. The song and the conversation move on to love.

‘Well I think that's in there and, yeah, I just happen to go through those conventional approaches to love. It is a very subversive position. Subversive is not quite the word...it's a radical position in that song that is beyond left and right. It talks about a reaction, an organic reaction, a convulsive reaction, that's not even a strategy or a plan of action, it’s just that you just can't tolerate the way things are. You can't lay the responsibility to the police or to the critics or to anything. But the whole song says there's a lie and because there's a lie it's going to die.

‘Who by Fire’ is one of Leonard Cohen's most simple songs, and a song that is drawn deeply from his Jewish background and it’s the song with which we finish the conversation. It’s a work that goes right down the line for everyone, a song about death. I wondered if he feared death himself.

‘I don't like the preliminaries. The actual event I'm not sure about one way or the other, but I sure don't like the preliminaries.’

‘Who by Fire’ is based on a prayer recited on the Jewish Day of Atonement. That prayer in itself has an interesting background. The popular story is that Rabbi Amnon, urged by the rulers of Mayence to change his faith, asked to be given three days to consider. When he failed to appear after the three days he was sought out and arrested. Forced to plead guilty, his hands and feet were cut off as a punishment. On the New Year, Rabbi Amnon was brought to the synagogue at his own request and recited the prayer-poem, 'Let Us Tell'. Having recited it, he died.

‘Well it's a great prayer. It's chanted in Hebrew on the Day of Atonement. The Day of Atonement is just one of the calendar holy days in the Jewish calendar and the most solemn day when you have to stand before the judge. And part of the liturgy that day is this recital of various ways you can leave this vale of tears. You know, some will go by fire, some by water, some by poisoning, some by hanging, some by drowning. So that's what it's about: who by fire, who by water. And I've just expanded on that into something maybe more complex, though that's plenty complex as it stands, that thousand-year-old prayer.

The prayer itself outlines the ways in which death can come calling.

On New Year, their destiny is inscribed and, on the Day of Atonement, it is sealed. How many shall pass away? And how many shall be brought into existence? Who shall live and who shall die?

Who shall come to a timely end and who to an untimely end? Who shall perish by fire and who by water? Who by sword and who by beast? Who by hunger and who by thirst? Who by earthquake and who by plague? Who by strangling and who by stoning? Who shall be at ease and who shall wander about? Who shall be at peace and who shall be molested? Who shall have comfort and who shall be tormented? Who shall become poor and who shall become rich? Who shall be lowered and who shall be raised? But repentance, prayer and charity cancel the stern decree.

Like the prayer, the song states the ways in which we may die and, like most of Cohen's songs, when listened to and absorbed, it cannot be dismissed as pessimistic or depressing. Its mood is one of hope; its style is one of beauty. Its importance is its relevance to everyone. It's written and sung with concern for the beggar on his crutch, the woman in the darkened door, the still-born child, the persecuted singer, the individual caught by the things he or she has done and can't undo. It's a summation of Cohen's belief. Here and now there is no conclusion, no reconciliation and no fulfilment. But beyond the dying, he maintains, there is a place where differences are reconciled, resolutions found. In a way, it's like his body of song: once you've crossed the bar, you find a relevance that you may never have expected.

~

The interview almost over, I returned to the subject of 'Song of

Bernadette.' The tape was still running.

'Have you ever recorded it?' I asked.

Leonard shook his head.

'Would you sing it for me now?' I asked.

'It's a grand song,' Leonard said. 'Let me see…'

He paused, recalling the words, and, as he did, the room door opened and the publicist stepped in.

'I'm sorry to interrupt,' he said, 'but we're way behind time, there are several other journalists waiting outside.'

'I'm really sorry, man. Another time.'

I pressed the stop button, gathered my notes, shook hands and left the room. Somewhere in the ether, Leonard's version of 'Song of Bernadette' had gone unsung.

Eight

The two-part documentary based on the interview I had done with Leonard, was broadcast on RTE Radio 1 in September 1988 under the title *How the Heart Approaches What It Yearns* – a line borrowed from a Paul Simon song.

The response was very positive and in 1989 I was awarded a Jacob's Radio Award for the programmes. I wrote to Leonard, thanking him for his work and giving him the good news. The reply came in the week of my thirty-seventh birthday.

Dear John,

Congratulations on the Jacob's Radio Award for this year. You certainly deserve it. I am glad I was part of the effort.

I am working on a bunch of new songs and they seem to be taking their time. It's good to hear from you. Please keep in touch.

Regards to your family,

Leonard Cohen.

If the award had been a welcome surprise, the letter was a treasure and, unknown to me, the first of many that would follow over the next twenty-seven years.

~

The Future, Leonard's ninth studio album, arrived in 1992, building on the success of its predecessor. It came in the wake of a period where Leonard had been away from music. His son, Adam, had been involved in a serious road accident that brought him close to death and Leonard had spent several months at Adam's bedside. Not surprisingly, music became a secondary consideration.

The Future was recorded in a range of studios with what can best be described as a medley of musicians. When the album arrived in the public marketplace, the reaction was universally positive.

The record opens with the title track – a song whose view of the world might, on an earlier collection, have qualified for a razor-blade nomination, referencing torture, lies, crack, anal sex, Stalin, St Paul, the Berlin wall, the devil's riding crop, fires on the road and foetal destruction and yet, in spite of all this, Leonard's sung response is that love is the only engine of survival.

The second track on the album, co-written by Sharon Robinson, is 'Waiting for the Miracle' and there's a line in the closing verse which pictures someone (I always see Leonard in my mind's eye and then I see the traveller in the story of the Good Samaritan) lying on a roadway in the rain. Someone passes and asks how he's doing and he ironically responds *can't complain*! It's like a moment from a Beckett play.

The tracks on *The Future* which particularly caught, held and continue to hold my attention are 'Light as the Breeze'; the winsome 'Tacoma Trailer' – an instrumental piece that closes the album – and 'Waiting for the Miracle.'

'Light as the Breeze' may be the greatest song ever written about oral sex but it is also an extraordinary companion piece to 'Our Lady of Solitude.' The female/goddess figure at the centre of the song might be an actual woman or a figurative representation of the feminine at the core of our lives, loves and experiences. Either way, the song is filled with spirituality, longing, confusion, contradiction and that wonderful image in the closing verse where Leonard writes of a blessing coming from heaven but only *for something like a second*. The sexual and spiritual high are there and then are gone. The mystic has his or her moment of enlightenment but such moments don't last and their disappearance – like the disappearance of Bernadette Soubirou's vision – leave a longing and an uncertainty in their wake.

The line reminds me of something Leonard once said about intimacy, about being able to physically but not emotionally reach across a bed.

Sometime after 'The Future' was released I finished the script of a play called *We Once Sang like Other Men*, the story of two characters (based on Peter and Mary of Magdala) who had been allies of a man called The Captain. It followed their lives and relationship in the wake of his execution. Years later I would expand the idea into a novel called *Once We Sang like Other Men* where twelve former comrades of The Captain would tell their versions of his story – the Jesus story.

The play toured with a cast of three and the music we chose for the show was 'Waiting for the Miracle' because that's what the characters in the play were doing, waiting for a miracle that would see The Captain reappear after his death.

What happens in the play is that things turn radically darker, leaving the three with memories of something they can never forget, something they wish they had never done in taking The Captain's words literally, following their last meal together.

The shadow that lies over the central characters' lives is mirrored in that song and it opened and closed the play – echoing the emptiness and uncertainty of those who find themselves adrift in the wake of loss.

'Tacoma Trailer,' the third track that intrigued me was, according to Leonard, intended as a piece of music for a theatre piece but, in the end, it became the closing track on *The Future*. 'A nice moment to unwind from a very dense and literate album.' The music in the piece is literary enough, summoning up images for me that are, sometimes, borrowed from *Paris, Texas* and come, sometimes, carrying images from Raymond Carver poems and stories. As it happens, Tacoma is in Washington State, Carver's long time home place.

I have often thought a theatre piece involving Ray Carver's poems and Leonard's songs would be enthralling – maybe someday.

~

The tour which followed the release of *The Future* didn't include Ireland and the price of the success of the album and the tour – which might have been an invitation to move on to bigger things – became the cornerstone on which Leonard based his decision to enter the Zen monastery at Mount Baldy, outside Los Angeles.

The Future tour was a mist of alcohol and depression for Leonard. He talked of needing four bottles of wine a day to keep pain and fear at bay – something that was unmanageable in the long term. The stage-fright he had experienced on his first appearance with Judy Collins seemed never to have gone away but was doubtless aggravated by his dependence on alcohol. In the face of his disillusion with fame, Mount Baldy and the Zen monastery seemed the better way.

~

Leonard had long been an admirer of the work and teaching of Kyozan Joshu Sasaki, better known as Roshi. Two years after his entry to the monastery, Leonard was ordained a monk and given the name Jikan (Silent One). He was almost sixty-four years old and he left behind a career that had just seen a second flowering.

At Mount Baldy, Leonard became the personal assistant to Roshi who had come to the United States in 1962 and founded a Zen centre in Los Angeles, going on to become Abbot of the monastery on Mount Baldy. He resigned from this position in 2012 at the age of 104. He died in 2014, leaving accusations of sexual exploitation of some of his students shading his reputation.

While at the monastery, Leonard's business affairs were left in the hands of his manager, Kelley Lynch. Over the years, I had a number of telephone conversations with her about matters to do with Leonard's tours, releases of albums and so on. She was always extremely pleasant and good-humoured to deal with and we chatted once or twice about her Irish roots – they had to be there with a name like hers. Leonard's decision to leave everything in her hands while he lived away from the world at Mount Baldy was to be the worst but, ultimately, for those who love his music, the most favourable of decisions.

~

Life on Mount Baldy was tough. The Zen Centre is a bleak spot, forty miles east of Los Angeles, more than six thousand feet above sea level, and the practice there was rigorous and demanding. Leonard writes about it in one of the poems published posthumously in *The Flame*. Among the things he notes about life at the monastery are the coldness, the darkness, the dangerous frost and snow, the inaccessibility, the food, the frozen drains, the swinging Zen gate (through which no one leaves) and the shovelling of snow. And then there were the hours spent in meditation, long hours. Why would Leonard want to be in a warm theatre playing to ten thousand people when he could, instead, be freezing on the side of a mountain and working as the monastery cook?

Leonard continued writing and composing during his monastic years. *Spring '96*, a documentary by the French film-maker Armelle Brusq, captures life on Mount Baldy. In the documentary Leonard talks about his decision to join the monastic life: 'I don't really know why I'm here. It's a matter of what else would I be doing? Do I want to be Frank Sinatra, who's really great, and do I want to have great retrospectives of my work? I'm not really interested in being the oldest folksinger around.'

Even the success of *The Future* and the tour that followed were hollow to a man who was still searching for the questions, before ever considering the answers.

Leonard described Mount Baldy as a waiting room, adding that the people there were sick and they wanted to see the doctor. The metaphor was a strong one. 'I was breaking down,' he said. He also talked about the sense of community in the monastery and how, when he lived in the world, a week or ten days would go by without his speaking to anyone. Life in Los Angeles was often, he said, 'a tyrannical solitude,' while the monastic life was 'communal and the contact with other people was refreshing for me.'

He portrayed his Zen master, Roshi, as 'the friend and the enemy… an enemy to your self-indulgence, a friend to your effort...he's going to be all the things he has to be in order to turn you away from depending on him. His love is a liberating kind of love.'

It seemed Leonard had found the ideal balance between love and the avoidance of over-familiarity, something that had troubled him all his life.

~

While Mount Baldy was a home from home for Leonard between 1994 and 1999, ultimately it wasn't the answer to his problems. The peace, the sense of community, the time and quietness to contemplate, to compose and create were all welcome aspects of the life. The late night drinking sessions with Roshi were another matter, a road back into the very darkness that had driven him to Mount Baldy in the first place. In an interview with National Public Radio, he said: 'It wasn't really addressing the problem – distress – which is the background for all my activities, feelings and thoughts. It was a lot of work for very little return…There were other feelings that are ambiguous and too difficult to describe. They deserve or probably should be described in song or poetry rather than conversation.' Eventually, some of those feelings would appear, posthumously, in 'Happens to the Heart.'

It seems to me, the relationship between Leonard and Roshi was one of the true, deep philosopher following a teacher.

~

Over the years Leonard spent at Mount Baldy, we kept in regular contact by email, exchanging birthday and Christmas and Jewish New Year greetings. Sometimes my catch up mails received an automatic reply, saying Leonard was out of circulation until the year's end – to be followed a day later by a response.

~

The experience of the monastery did, at the very least, give him direction and focus for his work. The practice of Zen monasticism was akin, in many ways, to the rigour of the creative process.

In his interview with Armelle Brusq, he said: 'You have to sit in that very bonfire of distress and you sit there until you're burnt away and it's ashes and it's gone ….and it's the same way with writing …some kind of sense of unbearable disorder in your own life, unbearable worthlessness, that drives you to take whatever you've got….a few things. You're searching in your pocket …maybe there's something there. It's the opposite of luxury. The operation is like rag picking…You finally come up with something that changes your mind about yourself, that changes your heart and creates a man around this song, around this poem.'

That last phrase resonates with me. Despite his man of the world persona, Leonard struck me as a very shy and diffident person. He expressed himself most clearly and most intensely in his songs and poems. I often think of him standing in a corner of the Richard Goodall gallery in Manchester, looking ill at ease as his fans and admirers flocked about him. There was something in that man, trapped in that busy gallery on a Sunday afternoon, wanting to be elsewhere, desiring to sit at his kitchen table and write, craving the opportunity to get on with the creation rather than the selling. And that image, in turn, reminds me of the story of his wanting, in the early years of touring, to wear a mask on stage.

Yes, he was a wonderful interviewee and, yes, he was highly articulate and observant. But the songs, the lyrics, the poems seem to me to be the places where we find the depth of his emotion and the poetic truth of his life and thought. The songs and poems are the centre around which his life held together. He was a true workman; that work was his expression of himself and it would continue right to the bitter end.

~

Leonard's return to the world, as the 1990s drew to an end, meant going back to the realm of music and production. Two years later, in 2001, he released the stunning *Ten New Songs*, co-written with Sharon Robinson. Much of the album was recorded in her garage. In Robinson – as in Patrick Leonard, years later – he had found an empathetic and considerate co-creator. There was none of the skulduggery of the Spector sessions.

'In My Secret Life,' which opens the album, is an astonishing exploration of the inside of one man's (and Every(wo)man's) heart and head – a song Leonard had been working on since the late eighties. For me, it nailed absolutely the contrast between how I am and how I'd like to be; between how I appear and how I feel; between the public shadow and the secret existence. And those contrasts are stark.

The more I listen to the song, the greater is the self-recognition. The lies, the deceptions, the failures of a lifetime are wrapped up in my own secret days and, yes, I would like to persuade myself that I, too, would die for the truth. But would I?

When Leonard writes about the dealers wanting us to see the world as black or white, I think of the pseudo-journalists, the influencers, the TV presenters, the politicians, the hucksters flogging their lines of all kinds and I sympathise with his observation that, at least in the secret life, there are grey areas and questions and uncertainties, there's a humanity that's missing from so much of what passes now for public discourse.

Having spent half a decade in the monastery at Mount Baldy, Leonard could still write about the coldness and the crowdedness in his secret life. The particulars may differ but in that lyric he has created an all-embracing anthem for humanity, matched by the allure of Sharon Robinson's music and vocals.

~

There's a small, wood-lined church at the Cistercian Abbey at Bolton Hill in Moone, Co Kildare. I worked as a gardener at the monastery for a couple of summers in my teens and I still visit on a regular basis for Compline. The sinking sun, in spring and summer, slants through the church's stained-glass windows, catching the motes of dust in the evening air.

When I first heard 'Love Itself,' it was the monastery church that came to mind – not just because of the dust motes but also because I often go there in search of spiritual consolation and calmness. I'm not a believer (or at best an agnostic one) but I find great solace in the sense of community and in the wisdom of the words I hear. And the singing of the 'Salve Regina' takes me back to other days and evening prayer in St Clement's school in Limerick.

Whether the little room in the song is Leonard's kitchen or his cabin on Mount Baldy doesn't matter. What is central is the convergence of emotion and matter; love and dust; a creative force and the naming of a man. Regularly, I find myself searching for a word with which to name my own state of mind, trying to locate a guiding purpose for my life.

Often, the moments of possibility disappear again when I step outside the monastery church, having, as Leonard says in the song, sporadically sensed the seldom grasped. But all that endure are the consequent moments when little remains beyond an uncertain recollection.

What does remain, however, are the words of the final blessing, from the Book of Numbers: 'The Lord bless you and keep you; the Lord make His face to shine upon you and be gracious to you; the

Lord turn His face toward you and give you peace.'

~

The other track on *Ten New Songs* which captured my imagination – not least because of Sharon Robinson's breath-taking delivery – was 'Alexandra Leaving' – based on a poem, 'The God Abandons Anthony' by the Greek poet Cavafy. In the poem, the Roman general Marcus Antonius is abandoned by the Gods before the disaster of Alexandria. And, of course, Antony is not only losing a battle but, also, his lover, Cleopatra.

In the song, Alexandria becomes Alexandra. The God who appears in Leonard's lyric is the God of love – Eros, the same God for whom the mountain that towers over Hydra is named. The lyric teems with longing but also regret. There is music and laughter and honour and kisses but there is, too, a recognition of a loss that might have been avoided.

That sense of waking and hoping the terror of a medical diagnosis or a personal betrayal were dreams, before the realisation of their realness strikes, is captured powerfully in the song – as is the fact that mostly we are the architects of our own downfall, the creators of our own disasters. Certainly, when I heard that song, I recognised those elements of myself within the lyric.

As *Ten New Songs* was being released, loss of a different kind was coming over the horizon, even if Leonard wasn't yet aware of its impending arrival.

Nine

The early years of the new century brought changes in my own life. In 2002, as I hit fifty, I took the decision to leave my job in RTE. I had been working there for twenty-three years and had thoroughly enjoyed the experience. I had worked in every department in radio – apart from sport and agriculture – but the most satisfying period was the time I had spent in religious programmes and the features and documentaries department.

There, I worked mostly on my own, interviewing, producing and presenting religious and book programmes and documentaries. I had been blessed with wonderful colleagues in RTE and with a line manager, John P Kelly, who encouraged the work I was doing. With the exception of one project, I had done everything I wanted to do and I felt it was a good time to move on.

Fulltime writing and a greater involvement in theatre, as a writer, director and actor, was the ambition but making a living was the necessity so I happily accepted some part-time work in the English and Adult Education departments at Maynooth University. That employment and occasional writing workshops kept the wolf from the door. Advances for my books just about paid for the safety bolt on the inside of the same door.

In 2004, Leonard released *Dear Heather* – an album he described as 'a kind of notebook or scrapbook of themes.' I was delighted to find one of my favourite poems, 'So, We'll Go No More a Roving,' by Lord Byron (a poem I'd long earmarked for reading at my own funeral) adapted by Leonard as the opening track. It was unwittingly apt, when you consider that Byron was probably inspired in his writing of the poem by the chorus of a Scottish song, 'The Jolly Beggarman.'

And we'll gang nae mair a roving
Sae late into the night,
And we'll gang nae mair a roving, boys,
Let the moon shine ne'er sae bright.
And we'll gang nae mair a roving.

Leonard, too, was on the way to losing a lot of money without realising it.

Byron's lyric reads:

So, we'll go no more a roving
So late into the night,
Though the heart be still as loving,
And the moon be still as bright.

For the sword outwears its sheath,
And the soul wears out the breast,
And the heart must pause to breathe,
And love itself have rest.

Though the night was made for loving,
And the day returns too soon,
Yet we'll go no more a roving
By the light of the moon.

I'd first encountered the poem in secondary school and its sense of lyrical beauty and romantic melancholia held a great appeal for a dreaming teenager, but it's an appeal that has never gone away because there's a profound truth in the work, a mood of deep resignation, matched by Leonard's delivery. The coupling of lyric, music and singer are perfect.

Another track on the album which engrossed me was 'The Faith.' It seemed to encapsulate so much of what Leonard talked of when we discussed religion, belief and charismatic holy men. The great images of cross, minaret and Davidian star are there but so, too, is the stark warning in the line about having so many graves to fill – in the name of religion, God, belief, faith or whatever pseudo-religious pennant or flag an army or an individual chooses to fly above the heads of the slaughtered and the maimed. Whether the love referred to is God or death, the world revealed in the words is bleak while the song itself is quietly beautiful.

Leonard's reference to wild regret is one of those phrases where his use of language, his employment of a totally surprising adjective reminds of his genius.

If the conversation Leonard is having in the song is with God, it foreshadows the conversations he will have in his final three albums. These exchanges are probing and, often, accusatory. He asks whether the other figure in the dialogue (referred to as *love*) is tired yet of filling graves?

The song closes by taking us back to the beginning, suggesting that the planet may end as it began, as a void created not for humankind but by humankind. We will, by then, have destroyed ourselves and our world.

~

The first hint I got of Leonard's financial situation came in the form of a long and rambling email from Kelley Lynch. It arrived in the weeks after my brother's death in the summer of 2005 and it took me a while to get around to reading it. The mail included copies of emails from others, including Phil Spector. The object of the exercise seemed to be to denigrate Leonard and, it appeared, Lynch was sending the mails in a scattergun attempt to blacken his name with anyone and everyone in her contact book.

In 1999, Leonard travelled to Bombay to study Vedanta, the Hindu philosophy, with Ramesh Balsekar. He would remain in India through 1999 and into 2000. Before leaving the United States, he had given power of attorney over his affairs to Kelley Lynch. What he didn't do, on his return, was to rescind that power and, so, Lynch had full control of his finances and now he was discovering that the monies he had saved for his retirement and to help his children with their lives were gone. Leonard was seventy years old and virtually all of his savings had disappeared.

I forwarded the mail, with my good wishes, to Leonard at the end of August and got a speedy reply thanking me for my note and assuring me that all was well. But, of course, all was not well. Leonard was heading into a seven-year period of threats to his life, abuse, litigation and severe stress. A couple of weeks later I sent Leonard a copy of Sheenagh Pugh's poem 'Sometimes' – a work that begins with the idea that sometimes things don't go from bad to worse. The poem goes on to suggest that sometimes crops grow; people step back from the brink, sun melts sorrow. My wish for Leonard was encapsulated in Sheena Pugh's line: 'may it happen to you.'

The reply came speedily:

dear John

thanks for the poem

all is well here

as i hope it is with you

warm regards,

L

(no final plans for a tour

just finishing a book and a record)

Leonard once described the process of song-writing as gathering 'pieces of bone and rag.' That description sat side by side with the line in 'If It Be Your Will' about all of us being here in our rags of light and it was one of the songs I chose to include in a 2007 production of a play I had written in the late 1990s called *Who by Fire* – a title, obviously, borrowed from Leonard's song. The first draft of the play was inspired by a number of poems I'd read by Holocaust victims and survivors. They were filled with images and stories which made an indelible impression on me.

I was aware of how the European Jewish population had been vilified over the centuries for everything from usury to the poisoning of wells. But the real root of my interest in the plight of that group went back to a school production of *The Merchant of Venice* in which I'd been cast, at my own request, as Shylock – a role I'd relished and a character I'd found myself defending to my classmates.

'You just love the underdog,' my English teacher remarked one day during rehearsals.

He was right. I saw the Jewish community of Shakespeare's time as underdogs.

The more deeply I read about the holocaust, the more I realised how other minorities had also been annihilated: gays; gypsies; Jehovah's Witnesses; those regarded as racially inferior, including people of African descent; non-conformists; vagrants; anyone who was not toeing Hitler's line. There was a manufactured excuse for the murder of every victim.

So the story of *Who by Fire* became the story of a Jewish family; of a gypsy; of two gay men, of the obliteration of those who were perceived as being different. It was a play about individuals caught in the brutality of the Holocaust.

In late 2006, I redrafted *Who by Fire*. The changes were inspired by the life and writing of Zoltan Zinn Collis, a survivor of Bergen-Belsen.

I had first met Zoltan when I landed a summer job as a waiter in Kilkea Castle Hotel. The year was 1970. Zoltan was the hotel chef but I knew nothing then of his past. The publication of his book *Final Witness* in 2006 inspired me to revisit and radically redraft the script I'd written, using Leonard's songs. The play went into rehearsal in January 2007 and Zoltan spoke with the cast on several occasions and was present at the premiere in February of that year.

The play – it was not a musical but a play with music – is the story of a woman who returns to Auschwitz in 1990, forty-five years after her release. Having lost her family in the camp – as Zoltan lost his – she comes face to face with the memories of her vanished kinfolk and the ghost of her younger self.

The play was not simply a staged event but rather a theatrical experience which began from the moment the audience arrived at the venue where they were stamped and segregated. For the premiere, the venue was a large and bitterly cold marquee, with a mound of several hundred pairs of shoes as the only set on a bare stage. Nor was there a barrier between actors and audience. Once the play began, the audience experienced what the performers were experiencing. Actors were removed from their seats in the auditorium to be stripped, de-loused and given prison garb. I was determined that there would be no fourth wall.

The songs – which Leonard had given his permission to use – were: 'Who by Fire;' 'First We Take Manhattan' (retitled 'First We Take the Reichstag,' with Leonard's agreement); 'Everybody Knows'; 'True Love Leaves No Traces'; 'The Future'; 'I'm Your Man'; 'Hallelujah'; 'Bird on the Wire'; 'Take This Waltz' and 'If It Be Your Will.'

The production company offered to fly Leonard to Ireland for the show but, by then, he was working on a new album. The week before the show opened a note arrived.

Dear John,

I wish you and the cast and the crew every success.

Leonard

Typical of Leonard, no one had been forgotten.

~

Who by Fire completed two sold-out national tours before transferring to Gibraltar. The stamping and segregation of audiences – women and children to the left; men to the right – often took theatre goers by surprise and on one occasion, at the Olympia Theatre in Dublin, a couple had a quite acrimonious argument (the irony being lost on them) as to who would get the box of chocolates they had brought to the show.

Reviews, with one exception, were positive:

The most compelling and powerful piece of theatre I have seen. It challenges and persuades and moves. You must see it.

A powerful re-enactment that leaves an indelible impression. Carefully handled with authenticity and pathos.

From the moment the audience entered, they found themselves part of this Auschwitz re-visiting.

A brave new piece of theatre, which implores the audience to become part of the event.

The scene in which the Polish prisoners are forced to strip naked in Auschwitz is as chilling as anything I've seen on stage. When Lotte and David duet on a pared-back version of 'True Love Leaves No Traces,' the song takes on a new meaning in the context of a couple facing oblivion, and when an unnamed prisoner (Adrian Sullivan) sings a heartbreakingly frail version of 'Bird on the Wire' with friend Charles (Declan McGauran) before execution, it's hard not to be moved. Likewise, silence descended on the auditorium as Jewish prisoners shuffled past a screen upon which the image of a flickering candle flame was projected while Sarah Maher sang the prayer-like 'If It Be Your Will'. And a standing ovation on its opening night suggested the audience found little to quibble with.

I forwarded the reviews to Leonard and the response came back immediately:

bravo! very happy for you and the cast
glad my songs could be of use
the standing ovation which transcends the entire critical establishment
congratulations L

~

Looking back at *Who by Fire*, I would make further changes to the script, tighten some scenes, probably drop one or two, but the emotion of the work, the power of the songs and the connection between cast, crew and audience made it something memorable and moving for everyone involved.

An afternoon in January 2007 stands out in my mind. We were

rehearsing in the sixteenth century White Castle in Athy. The building was cold and Zoltan Zinn Collis had called in to see how things were going. We took a coffee break and, as we sat together chatting, he told a story which deepened and darkened the chill in the freezing air. He recounted how, as his mother and his family waited to be loaded onto a train for Bergen-Belsen, a German soldier snatched his infant brother from Zoltan's mother's arms on the station platform and tossed the baby over a ten-foot wall and then the family was herded into a carriage and taken away.

I don't believe any member of the cast ever stepped onto a stage without remembering that baby.

~

When our tour ended, I was more than happy – given the financial woes in which he found himself – to be able to forward a healthy transfer for the performance rights of the songs to Leonard. *Thank you*, he wrote. *Much appreciated.*

As I read his mail, I recalled the first time we'd met and wondered how the hell someone so brilliant, trusting, generous and open-hearted had ended up losing virtually everything. And then it struck me – brilliant, trusting, generous, open-hearted: a recipe for exploitation.

~

Later that year, I travelled to Manchester for a preview of Leonard's art exhibition at the Richard Goodall Gallery. The gallery was thronged but we managed a very brief chat and I thanked him, again, for the permission to use the songs in the show. Leonard looked a little dazed and ill at ease. He was wearing that *I wish I were somewhere else* look. But the paintings and prints were selling.

The following week I received one of those concise missives that always brought a smile to my face:

good to see you, comrade

stay strong

love

L

~

My brother, Jarlath, had died in July 2005 and between his death and the summer of 2007 I had gone through a pretty dark time. Jarlath was ten years older than me and I always felt I had a guide in him, someone who had travelled much of the road I was travelling, someone I could call on for advice when times got rough.

In the two years following his death, the feeling of absence and darkness and uncertainty had deepened. I went through what might be labelled a mental breakdown. In Leonard I felt I had found another brother, someone to whom I could chat by mail about what was going on in my life. Sometimes the mails were about emotions, sometimes about songs or stories or poems I'd come across and, often, they were about my absent brother.

In late July 2007 I sent him a copy of Francis Ledwidge's poem

'To One Dead.' It was the ninetieth anniversary of Ledwidge's death and, in truth, the poem was as much an attempted consolation for myself as it was an introduction of Ledwidge's poems to Leonard.

~

Leonard had a deep love of the work of Lorca and of Yeats and I spent a couple of years trying to persuade him that Kavanagh was the Irish poet he should be reading. That was a battle lost. On his birthday that year I sent a copy of Kavanagh's poem, 'Advent' for which he thanked me but there was no concession on Yeats. Kavanagh's opening line in 'Advent' – about no wonder coming through a chink too wide – was, in its way, the inverse of Leonard's line about the crack in everything allowing the light in.

His response to my proposal of Kavanagh as the greater poet finished - as Leonard's letters often did – with a light-hearted observation:

thanks John (they'll never get us)

~

A second tour of *Who by Fire* followed in the autumn of that year. During the tour, I was approached by the director of an arts festival, wondering whether Leonard would consider reading at their event the following year. It wasn't the first time I'd been asked to put in a request and I had a pretty good idea what the response would be but I agreed to make enquiries. The suggested fee was a healthy one and I thought the cash might be a help in straitened times.

My mail to Leonard arrived on the same day that the money from the second run of *Who by Fire* landed in his account. The reply was, as I had guessed it would be.

John

Thanks for the bread. Much appreciated.

Have no idea where I'll be next year, maybe on a world-wide tour; so I'll have to pass on the generous invitation. A handsome fee, and a gracious invitation but I'm afraid I can't make it.

Happy (Jewish) New Year!

Leonard

The courteous refusal didn't at all surprise me but the possibility of an upcoming tour grabbed my attention and raised the anticipation level.

~

On November 30th – the fortieth anniversary of Patrick Kavanagh's death, I sent another of his poems, 'Epic', to Leonard – this time there was a slight concession:

...lifting a glass to PK.

Ten

The Kilmainham concerts of June 13, 14, 15 2008 were extraordinary. The setting was inspiring. I found myself sitting beside a couple, on the third night, who intended following Leonard across Europe and going to all of his shows.

I had asked Leonard whether he would like to take a couple of hours off, to visit Newgrange, but he was committed to sound-checks. On the road, the concerts were everything. And, when I think about it, now that I'm seventy, he was a man of 73 preparing for a series of three-hour concerts. Interesting as Newgrange might be, it was a mad idea. I had done a ten week tour with a play that spring and I was jaded. I couldn't begin to imagine how demanding and wearing a world tour would be, involving three-hour performances night after night.

I did chance my arm a little farther, attempting to undo the missed opportunity of all those years before in Jury's Hotel, by asking Leonard whether he'd consider singing 'Song of Bernadette.' He graciously pointed out that the band and he hadn't rehearsed it.

~

I always felt there were elements of every Leonard concert and album and poetry collection that were provocative – in the sense that they stimulated, confronted and challenged, if only through a sardonic point of view or an unexpected tackling of something that might otherwise seem hackneyed. For me, that element of surprise and provocation was there, right back to 'Story of Isaac.' And it was still there on Leonard's, then, most recent album *Dear Heather* in a song like 'Undertow,' where he used the remarkably tender image of a heart in the shape of a begging bowl. In eight words, he created a reflection that was at once deeply poetic, challenging in its imagery, spiritual and human in its significance and as wonderfully appropriate as it was unexpected. If our hearts are begging bowls, what does that say about us, about our relationships and about the human circumstance?

~

Afterwards, Leonard would talk about how warm and welcoming the Kilmainham reception had been and how it almost brought him to tears on stage. He spoke about glancing at the guitar player, at one point, and there were tears streaming down his face.

Kilmainham truly was a demonstration of the love of the people. There had been tributes and covers and albums by other singers but here was the man, the poet, the composer, the singer delivering an extraordinary performance, committing himself, again, to the songs and the listeners. If there were tears on stage, there were tears, too, in the audience And dancing in the aisles and flowers being thrown onto the stage and too much alcohol and – something I just don't understand – people falling drunkenly asleep in their seats but, most of all, there were the songs, alive and deep and beautiful – from 'Dance Me to the End of Love' to 'Whither Thou Goest.' As I listened and watched I was reminded of a mail I'd received from Leonard earlier that year, before the tour dates were finalised. I'd been wondering whether he'd perform in Ireland. He had been emphatic in his reply: *Yes, we'll be playing Ireland, of course*. As if the question didn't need asking.

~

In 2009, I was approached, again, by a Festival organiser who hoped Leonard might be interested in reading from his work and wondering whether I would make contact. I did, apologizing for the intrusion and already knowing the answer but aware, too, that it wasn't my place to presume to speak on his behalf. The reply came, as ever, with courtesy:

Dear John,

Thanks for the invitation, but I'll be touring with this band all through 2009, and maybe longer. We're just going to keep going, G-d willing, performing and recording, as long as we can. We'll be in Asia, then N. America, most of next year.

Thanks for thinking of me.

Warm regards, L

~

On Leonard's seventy-fourth birthday, I sent him some lines from Mary Oliver: 'Instructions for living a life.' In the poem she urges the reader to pay attention, to be open to astonishment and to tell others about it.

Not that I thought that he needed instructions from me – or Mary Oliver – but the lines seemed to sum up what he had been doing so well for so long.

~

Leonard had always been generous and encouraging with his permissions for use of lyrics and I approached him, again, with an enquiry about the use of a verse from 'Night Comes On' in a novel of mine, *The Space between Us*, which was due from New Island books. Where other writers would sometimes redirect requests to publishers and agents, Leonard was never less than unstinting in his responses.

The song appears in the book at a point where the narrator, whose only daughter has been murdered, turns on the radio in the middle of the night and catches a verse of the song. The verse that begins: 'I look for her always…'

It seemed particularly apposite, given that the relationship between father and daughter had been intense. The imagery in that verse is like something out of *Wuthering Heights*, filled with other-worldliness but also with a deep and compulsive connection between the living and dead, one that tears down the curtain between the two worlds.

~

I regularly used Leonard's lyrics in my Maynooth University writing workshops and, inevitably, they drew strong opinions and initiated intriguing discussions. On one occasion, at a weekend workshop, a healthy debate grew from the lyrics of 'Ballad of the Absent Mare.' Opinions were divided on the subject and the Saturday afternoon discussion ran on for almost an hour. So, I thought I'd go to the source and ask some questions of Leonard, hoping I might have an answer for the following week's session. Instead, the reply came by return, outlining that it's *based on an ancient Chinese series of woodblocks called "Ten Ox-Herding Pictures" a standard text in Zen studies*. Not only that, there was a link to the illustrated passages and a note wishing the workshop group all the best.

The surprise, on the Sunday morning, when the information and link were available, courtesy of the writer himself, was palpable. And, as so often, Leonard's generosity with his time and knowledge was openhearted to a fault.

~

Towards the end of 2009, I got a short note from Leonard. We had been chatting about his planned tour, due to start the following March. He said he believed he'd be *back in my cave by the summer of 2010*. As it happened, spinal trouble, which was successfully treated (and which saw Leonard embark on a Pilates course) meant the tour was postponed to July 2010. By then, Leonard was seventy-five, remarkably fit and enthusiastic for the road.

~

That Christmas, I sent an e-card to friends, Leonard among them, with a lyric inspired by the memory of childhood Christmases in Castledermot and the fact that so many of the figures who peopled those memories were now dead. The piece was called 'The Ghosts of Christmas Past.' It read, in part:

We meet them only at this time of year,
their warm, lost smiles come shining once again,
they step out from our memory
like rainbows in the rain.

A scent that was the scent of life returns,
darkness dissolves, old songs drift in the night air,
a dream becomes a tender touch,
frost lights your ghostly hair.

And, if I listen, I can hear your words
and say the things I never chanced to say.
Belief becomes an absolute,
for this short, winter day.

Leonard's reply came on midwinter day:

beautiful
thank you
keep warm
love
L

Eleven

In early 2010 the news broke of the planned concerts at Lissadell in Sligo. Leonard was coming out of a period of recuperation and, according to a letter I got from him, *running close to the edge*.

~

The weather forecast for the nights of the Lissadell concerts was, to put it mildly, not promising. On the morning before the first show I dropped him a line:

Leonard

Welcome to a slightly damp island.

Greatly looking forward to tomorrow night's concert.

Though with the weather forecast we may need one Canadian (canoe) to see another!

In the middle of the Sligo mayhem, he made time to reply:

Thanks, John. Fraternal greetings

~

Leonard's Sligo sojourn included a trip to Drumcliffe cemetery and church to visit the grave of W. B. Yeats and to sign the visitors' book, *Leonard Cohen, Montreal.* The weather in Lissadell lived up, or down, to expectations with everything from rain to a clear, clean moonlit sky. The concerts themselves – the setting; the Yeats connection; the sight and sound of the ocean in the background; the set-list from 'Dance Me to the End of Love' to 'Lover, Lover, Lover,' with a Yeats' poem included – were particularly special evenings.

The ghosts who lingered in the shadows might have wondered at the event but the audience, who sat or danced through the rain and the then beneath the clearing skies, soaked up every moment of all that was offered by Leonard and the band.

Sharon Robinson later remarked that the gigs in Sligo were among Leonard's favourites.

Wonderful – and typical – stories emerged. Backstage, the crew and musicians had to sign-in before having their meals. The signing-in included a name and who the person was working for. Leonard joined the queue for food and signed the book: 'Leonard Cohen. Working for myself.'

On the Saturday of the concerts, Leonard issued an invitation to all of the people working on site to sit and enjoy the eighty minute sound-check if they so wished. A couple of dozen souls took up the offer, scattered among the more than thirteen thousand seats, enjoying their own, private recital.

~

What I didn't know on that Saturday night, July 31, as I sat, drenched by the rain and the music, was that an acquaintance, who was also at the concert, had suffered a brain haemorrhage and been removed to hospital.

It was only in the weeks following the event that I got to hear the news. I mentioned it in passing to Leonard. He sent me a message by return, hoping it wasn't the music that had brought on the illness, and asking that a message be passed on to my, thankfully, recovering acquaintance. It read:

Dear M- H-,
Thank you for coming to the concert in Sligo.
What a beautiful place it is!
I hear from my friend John that you've been a bit under the weather,
but that you're feeling better now. I send you my very best wishes.
Love and blessings,
Leonard

~

From Sligo, Leonard travelled to Malmo and the tour continued for more than fifty nights, journeying across Europe and then on to New Zealand, Australia, Canada and the United States, finishing in Las Vegas in the second week of December.

In a letter, sent while he was on the road, Leonard wrote:

John,

When this tour finishes at the beginning of next year,

I'll be hiding out for a while, probably with my old teacher,

Roshi, who is 103.

Impossible to make plans beyond that.

All the best

L

~

On a night in mid-December 2010, I was sitting at my desk. At that time I was living in an apartment that overlooked a cemetery and a railway yard. I was listening, as I often did when I wrote, to *Various Positions.* There had been extraordinarily heavy snow for days and, as I worked, I noticed car lights moving slowly along the narrow path between the graves and then stopping. An elderly couple alighted from the car and began to clear the snow from a grave. This was repeated the following night and every night until the snow melted.

One afternoon I visited the grave and discovered it was the burial place of a young man. The couple, I assumed, were his parents.

What I saw reminded me of the opening lines of 'Night Comes On.'

I wrote to Leonard, telling him what I'd witnessed. It seemed an expression of the saddest and finest elements of humanity. It transpired, coincidentally, as Leonard told me, that he had just reintroduced 'Night Comes On' into his touring set list.

~

Letters between us in 2011 were sporadic. In August, Leonard wrote that he was *completely out of the loop*. In September I sent him a copy of Mary Oliver's poem 'Why I Wake Early' by way of celebration of his birthday:

John

thank you so much for your greeting and the beautiful poem

much appreciated

Leonard

~

My friend Richard Ball – with whom I'd spent those Cohen-reading-and-listening summers in London – contacted me with a poem about Leonard, written by an eighteen-year old student of his, Conor Farnan. It was a strong and mesmerising work and I forwarded it to him.

The interested sitting

Leonard, old man oral scribe, I sit obsessed by what you do;
old man who took me to his apartment on a heavy Greek evening,
with sun spilling cool on whitewashed walls
& opened his shirt three buttons down,
ready to swim in the cosmic mix at all cost,
who abandoned me in McDonalds, O Connell St, bloated,
gazing into cold coffee as if to pray!

who serenaded my beautiful immaturity and drank deep,
feasting on the skin when I hung on those sentences,
who taught me by sensual demonstration to make love easily
to the shy and teasing naked air beside my stereo,
who sang with such purpose of transmission of the fact
of the emptiness of all human joy
and who gave in replacement the lyrics of pure absent company
& the gift of the realisation that my mad mother would be OK,
he whom I sensed in his real holy breath
laying down his lazy melody upon my
shoulders like some holy mantle,
droning in seventy-year-old groans for me to
go & preach peace within my Self -
Leonard, when your lips tilt to the mic
and long-nailed fingers tease the strings
of that eternal guitar, the gates of Hell appear,
opened wide, and they are welcoming.

Leonard wrote back to say how good he thought it – *damn good and much appreciated.*

~

At Christmas 2011 I included with my Christmas card Robert Frost's 'Dust of Snow.' In the course of his reply, Leonard wrote: *and some dust of snow to you too, brother. L.*

~

In April 2012 the Kelley Lynch situation was temporarily resolved when she was sentenced to a term in prison. In his summation, Judge Vanderet said that the "evidence demonstrated in this case a long unrelenting barrage of harassing behaviour on the part of the defendant that spanned a number of years and was really vile...no person should be subject to that kind of targeting by anyone and that's why we have statutes in place to prevent that." He also acknowledged that Lynch "displayed an utter contempt for the judicial process and for judicial orders" and had shown "no remorse or glimmer of acknowledgement of wrongdoing for her behaviour."

In his victim impact statement, Leonard was gracious and caustic. Having thanked the court and the public prosecutor who had handled the case he went on to thank Kelley Lynch's legal team for 'their restraint in presenting only a portion of the material they knew was untrue.' He thanked Kelley Lynch for insisting on a jury trial, thus allowing the public to see 'her massive depletion of my retirement savings and yearly earnings.' He spoke glowingly of his attorney: 'I would like to read into the public record my gratitude to my attorney Ms Michelle Rice. Without her meticulous attention to a staggering volume of material, we would not be here today, and the full extent of Ms. Lynch's deliberate cruelties and evasions would not be known. It is through Ms. Rice's pains-taking management of these toxic details ...that we were able to present the case.' He concluded: 'It gives me no pleasure to see my one time friend shackled to a chair in a court of law...It is my prayer that Ms Lynch will take refuge in the wisdom of her religion, that a spirit of understanding will convert her heart from hatred to remorse, from anger to kindness, from the deadly intoxication of revenge to the lowly practice of self reform.'

Kelley Lynch was sentenced to eighteen months in jail for harassment, followed by a five-year probation period and ordered to undergo anger management, alcohol and psychiatric counselling while in jail.

But the reprieve from that harassment would only be a temporary one. On her release, Lynch resumed her persecution of Leonard with a barrage of emails. As late as July 2016, she sent him 39 mails over a three day period, in direct contravention of court orders.

Just eight weeks before his death, and at a time when he was seriously ill, Leonard would be interviewed by a detective investigating Lynch's ongoing violations of the court order not to harass him.

Lynch would be indicted a second time, after Leonard's death, for continued harassment of his manager, Robert Kory, and his attorney, Michelle Rice.

~

But, in 2012, there was the temporary respite of her being in jail. Knowing Leonard would be in Dublin in September for three concerts and knowing I had a collection of poems – *Where Sadness Begins* – going out into the world at that time, I asked whether he might consider attending the launch, if the timelines fitted.

As ever, the reply was considerate and interesting:

Dear John,

I wish I were the kind of guy who could do that kind of thing,

but I'm not.

I never see anyone or go anywhere between concerts,

and even when I'm not on tour

I'm mostly confined to barracks.

My friends put up with me not going to their concerts,

or openings, or launches, or even dinner parties.

I rarely leave my house or my neighbourhood.

I think it was Yeats' father who said,

Poetry is the social act of a solitary man.

Something like that. The concert is my social life.

I go from the stage directly to my hotel room,

and I stay there until the next sound check.

I hope you will forgive me.

I'd very much like to have your book.

It looks like the real thing.

Love,

Leonard

I replied that I blamed Yeats' father, not only for Leonard's not attending the book launch but also for the parlous state of the world economy and the Irish weather.

~

September 11, 12 and 13 2012, saw Leonard playing, again, at IMMA. The night I was there was a bitterly cold one but, from first word to last note, the show was a marvel. The tour came on the back of the *Old Ideas* album, which had been released at the beginning of the year.

The tracks on that album which most drew me in were 'Crazy to Love You,' which Anjani Thomas had co-written and recorded on her *Blue Alert* album. From the moment I heard Anjani sing it; I hoped Leonard would record it, too. It has a lyric that's filled with the yearning and the experience of a lifetime. The third verse is so full of the human circumstance – the personal and the general – that I wish I had heard it when I was twenty. When Leonard sings the song, I can feel the tiredness and the quiet satisfaction of what he calls a blessed fatigue. And there's the sardonic humour in there about being older and the mirrors not lying.

'Going Home' and 'Amen,' the first and second tracks on the collection are laced with sadness and regret – but 'Going Home' is spiked, too, with humour and has elements of a comedian conducting his own funeral service.

'Amen' is a much darker, unleavened affair. It travels through a catalogue of imagery that touches on alcohol abuse; remorse; vengeance; butchery; the blood of the lamb and the Holocaust camps. And, as with so many of Leonard's images, the vision of angels *scratching* at the door is as inspired as it is unsettling.

The other song on that album which I immediately loved and have grown to love and appreciate even more is 'Come Healing,' with music by Patrick Leonard.

On first hearing, I was drawn to the spiritual imagery – the abandoned cross; the penitential hymn; the gates of mercy – but, as time passed and circumstances changed in my own life, I began to see and hear a different aspect of the lyrical experience.

In 2021, without any real warning, I was told I needed a triple coronary artery by-pass. There were no obvious symptoms but the work needed to be done quickly. As I sat in my hospital room on the night before the operation, I seriously considered doing a runner and taking my chances. I had even begun to repack my bag when, in the space of an hour, two visitors arrived (this was after 10 pm).

The first was Chris Jacques, my wife's former husband, who works in theatre in the hospital. He talked me through the operation and left me feeling more optimistic about my chances.

The second was retired Bishop Éamonn Walsh who was working as chaplain in the hospital. We sat and talked about life and death and Leonard, not surprisingly made an appearance in the conversation. By the time Éamonn left, with a promise that he'd see me in recovery (which he did) I was a lot calmer.

When I was alone, I found a live recording of 'Come Healing' on YouTube and listened to it over and over. The lines about the longing of the arteries to purify the blood were particularly apposite, given my condition.

Leonard appeared, again, three nights later in a bizarre dream where my wife, Angela; Leonard and myself were in a coffee shop somewhere in Clare when we met the piper and composer Brian Hughes. By the time we'd finished our coffee we had arranged to tour a show called *Celtic Cohen*. Brian would play Leonard's music on the pipes and we'd intersperse poems and readings between the songs. The odd thing was that, although we were chatting to Leonard, we all knew he couldn't be part of the tour because he was dead. As the dream came to an end, we agreed that the best place to stage these performances would be in bookshops and then off Leonard went, drifting down the coffee shop stairs and gently fading into nothingness.

~

But on that September night in 2012, Leonard was very much alive. President Michael D Higgins told me, years later, that he went backstage to meet Leonard after one of the IMMA gigs and found him eating chicken soup. Leonard offered his cup to the President and they shared the meal.

I do remember that the weather was cold in Kilmainham once the sun dipped. Warm and all as stage lights were, I felt a deep sympathy for the seventy-five-year-old Leonard (and the band) as the night deepened and the temperature fell. A note from Leonard on the following day read:

dear John

thank you for braving the weather L

~

In October, as I hit my fifty-eighth birthday, Leonard sent one of his droll mails by way of congratulation:

Dear John

Sending you the very happiest Birthday Wishes!

It gets easier from now on, I promise you.

All the blessings, Leonard

~

That autumn, as I taught creative writing to first year undergraduates at Maynooth University, we were discussing literature and spirituality and I turned the students' attention to Leonard's collection of prayers and psalms, *Book of Mercy*. One of the students, an eighteen-year old, said: "My mother loves Leonard Cohen." The young woman beside her leaned across the table and added: "Never mind your mother, *I* love Leonard Cohen."

I told the story to Leonard and he laughed and asked that I *thank her for the encouragement*.

I did.

~

Book of Mercy, published in 1984 has been a constant companion to me for forty years. I'm on my seventh copy, having given the other six away. It's not an easy book but it's beautiful. Written in his fiftieth year, it contains fifty psalms or prayers. Leonard described it as 'a secret book for me…a little book of prayer…only valuable to someone who needs it.' He also described it as 'a sacred kind of conversation.'

In an interview on CKUA he said '(it's) a book of prayer…unless you have no other recourse...this book couldn't possibly have significance for you...For me it wasn't just useful but urgent….It was a pressing need to speak and it was a pressing need to address myself to the source of things and that's what the book is about. And now it's over and I'm just the same messy character I always was. There's no conversion…I'm not evangelical about it. But that is the record of how a heart was shattered and unified.'

The image of the unified heart is one to which Leonard regularly returned – visually and verbally.

Pressed by the interviewer, Tony Dillon Davis, to explain, Leonard said: 'Oh it hurts, it hurts. Everyone has their own tiny domain of suffering…and there are moments that are unmanageable and when you are silenced and when the taste goes out of things…and a great silence comes down…In moments like that, many people find solace in their own traditions as I did…This is the work of a civilian of the spirit…it's not a prescription.'

He went on to talk about the influence of the poets Rumi and Attar, the Sufi poets, on his work and their importance as sources of light and he warned, in a wonderful phrase, that they should only be approached 'if you feel your soul unemployed.'

He also talked about the tradition of questioning God – a practice he would return to in his final three albums.

Twelve

In the autumn and early winter of 2012, I was struggling with the novel I was writing. In a letter from that period I wrote to Leonard:

I happened to stumble across an interview you did with a journalist from Norwegian TV - back in 2006.

Having watched it, and before getting back to the &$+&!% novel, which is proving troublesome beyond trouble, I just wanted to drop you a line and say how much I enjoyed the interview and how often I go back to Book of Longing and Book of Mercy – and how it struck a chord when you talked about a book being a small thing in the great scheme of things – yet we plough on with our work, trying to produce something that might say something; hoping the next one will speak in an even vaguely original voice; perhaps (in my case) hoping to leave one more book that might act as an echo in years to come....*

The novel I was working on would, finally, see the light of day in 2014. It was called *Joseph* and was a retelling, set in contemporary times, of the story of Joseph, the step-father of Jesus – or was he? Joseph is a character who has long fascinated me, a character with a bit part in the Jesus story but one with great possibilities when it came to fiction.

In the novel, Joseph is a small time builder. His step-son – 'the young fellow' – is his wife's child but there's a strong bond between Joseph and the boy. Joseph's love of music provides the chapter titles and he's one of the characters I'm most fond of as a person.

The book would be dedicated to Leonard and to John Macdougald, a friend and former GP. Between them, they had, as the dedication says, kept me afloat spiritually and physically in the darkest of times.

~

We had moved house in May 2012 and were in the throes of decorating, buying furniture, settling into a new life and paying a mortgage – something neither of us had been burdened with for more than a decade. Money was tight and when Leonard's concerts were announced for the O2 Arena in September we sat down and looked at the financial situation and decided we'd have to pass on that particular outing.

In July I sent a copy of my new poetry collection to Leonard and promised to send a copy of *Joseph* when it appeared. Leonard's note regarding the books reminded me of his comment, all those years before, when we recorded the *Favourite Five* programme – about losing things:

Dear John,

Thank you - I'd like to have your books.

Post is best.

I lose everything on the road.

No hurry, because I don't really get back home until the end of the year (Dec 20th, I think).

Very kind of you.

L

The road, it seemed, would go on forever.

~

On a warm morning in July 2013, I turned on my computer to find a mail from Leonard asking to me contact Mike Scoble, his tour manager, to arrange complimentary tickets for Angela and myself for the September show. I have no idea what kind of intuitive affinity made Leonard get in touch but, suddenly and out of the blue, we were going to see him on September 12. Gratitude doesn't describe the feeling we had and I'm sure our new neighbours wondered about the whooping and yelling that escaped through our open summer windows.

~

The concert in Dublin was charged with anticipation and enthusiasm. None of us who were there knew whether this would be Leonard's last Irish show but there was a palpable sense, an intuitive folk consciousness that it might be the time and place to say thanks and adieu.

As it happens, Leonard went onstage that night with renewed energy and with the ambition of there being at least one further tour before he called it a day. Whatever *our* collective intentions were in bidding farewell, they were absolutely not Leonard's.

The seats we'd been assigned were the best we'd ever had. As we sat waiting for the show to begin, I couldn't help thinking about that night, more than forty years earlier, when I'd stood at the side of the food van in the National Stadium and chanced my arm to see Leonard a second time.

People say the Kilmainham gigs were special and they were. Sligo had its own beautiful magic but for me, and this is not written in the glow of hindsight, that night in September 2013 had an atmosphere I had never experienced at a Leonard concert. And it wasn't simply about this, perhaps, being the last time we'd see and hear him. The concert was too full, too lively, too musically and lyrically driven to allow that possibility to dominate. There was an energy that spoke of life and love and living and dancing and listening and hearing new things in the old ideas, new views in the old pictures and new wonders in the breadth of the songs, from 'Dance Me to the End of Love' to the last extraordinary notes of Doc Pomus and Mort Schuman's 'Save the Last Dance for Me.'

The night began and ended with dances, as life does – the dance of birth to, as Jackson Browne wrote, *the dance we all must do alone.* For almost four hours, the life of one man spooled out before us – the darkness, the healing, the fire, the leaving, the secret life and the closing time.

And, when he sang, 'Save the Last Dance for me,' he stood back from the microphone, beaming, while the audience sang: 'Leonard, save the last dance for me.'

I wrote to him the following day, thanking him for the tickets and telling him how much I loved the show:

God was alive and magic was afoot last evening. So many highlights - among them a reading of 'Lover, Lover, Lover' that I'd never connected with before; 'The Partisan,' which sent a series of shivers down my spine because I was hearing it afresh, as the bold but bitterly sad anthem for so many lost souls in so many conflicts; 'Alexandra Leaving'; 'If It Be Your Will' - if you never wrote another word, 'in our rags of light, all dressed to kill' would say it all. I had a friend who died this year, he spent the first six years of his life in Auschwitz - he talked of playing hide and seek on piles of bodies as liberation day drew near - and he loved that song, though sometimes it took away his ability to articulate what was in his heart and left him, literally, speechless.

On a brighter note – 'Going Home' took me to a revival meeting somewhere in Mississippi - but without the supposedly vengeful God lurking outside the tent; 'A Thousand Kisses Deep' always throws up things that are new and frighteningly real. Oh and that line about the full length mirror ... have you considered stand-up comedy?

And then...the first single my brother ever brought home, 'Save the Last Dance for me'...enough said.

I can't wait for the concerts when you really get into your stride in your eighties.....

A reply came two days later from London and ended warmly with:

thank you, brother

love and blessings

L

~

Christmas 2013 brought a good wish card and a note:

John,

Did I ever thank you for the books you sent? I did read your very beautiful poems.

Much appreciated.

Fraternally,

L

Thirteen

February 8, 2014. Another of those mornings when I turned on my computer and there was a message I really hadn't expected. It was from Robert Kory, Leonard's manager, asking whether I would be willing to write the sleeve notes for the CD/DVD of Leonard's Dublin concerts. I was dumbfounded and my initial reaction was that this was a set-up by one of my friends.

But I reread the email, including Robert's line about leaning on the relationship Leonard and I had, and I immediately thought of all the times – knowingly and unknowingly – that I had leaned on Leonard's music, lyrics, poems, friendship and good advice.

I immediately rang Angela. I don't think she believed me but, by the time she'd got back to the house, I had replied to Robert telling him I'd be honoured to write the liner notes.

Once I received Robert's second mail – a confirmation that the request was genuine – I got to work on the notes. There were many, many things I wanted to include and the first few drafts ran to thousands of words but, day by day, I whittled the word count down and focused on the things I needed to include. I wanted the piece to be personal but I also wanted to acknowledge and honour the tremendous warmth that existed between Leonard and his Irish fans. I'm not even sure *fans* is the right word – enthusiasts; devotees; admirers; disciples in some cases; self-admitted fanatics, in the best sense. *Comrades* is, perhaps, the best word I can find, comrades in song.

To listen as he thanked people for being at the O2 in 2013 and to hear his recognition of the financial hardship many of the audience were going through – and his acknowledgement of the many who could not afford to be there – was to appreciate that the comradeship was reciprocated.

When he spoke that evening about the economic and emotional strain many people were under I was reminded of his words during his acceptance speech at the Prince Asturias Awards. On that October night in 2011 he said: 'Just as an identity card is not a man, a credit rating is not a country.' Leonard was politically knowledgeable enough to know that Ireland was, with Portugal, Greece and Spain lumped under the acronym PIGS – a label slapped on four countries driven to economic and human despair by those who conceitedly told us they knew what they were doing.

As I listened to Leonard that September night in the O2, I was reminded of the words of his friend Judy Collins in her song 'Che.'

You have it in your hands to own your own life, to own your own land.

There is no one who can show you the road you should be on,

they only tell you they can show you and then tomorrow they are gone.

~

All of these ideas and memories were swirling in my head as I redrafted the sleeve notes. Yeats was there and the deep spirituality of Kavanagh; and Paul Durcan and Denis O'Driscoll with their unique views on humanity; and Mary Oliver with her gentle mysticism; and Jackson Browne and Joan Baez and Judy Collins and Pete Seeger with their roots in the folk songs of Leonard's earliest musical experiences; and Michael Gorman with his take on a Sligo that differed radically and quietly from the Sligo of which Yeats had written; and Theo Dorgan who would, in time, create an extraordinarily beautiful poem on Leonard.

In the end, I got the word count down to what was required. As always with short pieces, much of what I wanted to say and many of those I wished to put shoulder to shoulder with Leonard had, sadly, disappeared after the first, second and third drafts

I sent the finished piece to Robert. He came back very quickly, asking whether I was happy to have it sent to Leonard? I was.

And then I waited.

Our wedding day was less than two weeks away and the plans were at full throttle but I was aware that I might well have to rewrite the whole thing or, worse still, that Leonard might decide it wasn't what he had in mind.

I didn't have very long to wait. Another mail from Robert:

Just finished a meeting with Leonard. His comment..."just right...excellent." He suggested "About Leonard" as a title.

~

Later that year *Live in Dublin* appeared as a double CD and DVD, recorded on September 12, 2013, the night Angela and I had been there as Leonard's guests. And there were the sleeve notes:

It's the summer of 1971. I'm eighteen years old, have just finished my first year in college and I'm working on a building site when I fall into the arms of meningitis. It ambles with me to death's door but the gate is locked and bolted. In the weeks that follow, my sister's friend loans me two LPs – Songs of Leonard Cohen and Songs from a Room. They play constantly in the darkness and they reawaken me, giving me a glimpse of the world, giving me an inkling of the possibilities of the word.

It's March 13th, 1972, I see Leonard for the first time, in the old National Boxing Stadium in Dublin – a tired, shabby building that takes on new life this spring evening. He does two shows – I have a ticket for the first but manage to pass myself off as one of the catering staff for the second. He sings the Irish ballad Kevin Barry and the hackneyed standard of pub rebels becomes something new again, something electric and exhilarating. And, on visit after visit to these shores, Leonard fortifies us and intrigues and warms us with his affection and his loyalty.

He becomes a part of who we'd like to be; a voice when we are voiceless; a soul when we doubt ourselves. He is the singer on the stage at Lissadell, quoting Yeats as the night comes on, and he's a friend at the kitchen table.

And there's something even deeper that connects us – the spirit in his work. When he sings If It Be Your Will, we recognise the ghosts of our own famine millions in the souls lost in the Holocaust; when Isaac's father opens the door, we are nine-year-olds in the shadows of love and uncertainty; we know the drunk in the midnight choir, we've heard his fractured song; we connect with the Catholicism of Leonard's city and with the Judaism of his imagery, because these are the symbols on which we were raised. And we love the fact that he came to Ireland at times when no one else was coming – through the bad days and the good and then, again, the bad. When he tells us, at the 2013 concerts, that he appreciates our buying tickets when budgets are tight, we know he understands the situation.

And, of course, his honesty and his humour ring bells with us – when he sings 'Mother, I'm frightened, the thunder and the lightning...' he might be a child in a Frank O'Connor short-story; the woman whose dress was blue and silver, whose words were few and small could so easily be a character in a John McGahern novel and the close companion who's a hundred but wearing something tight might have stepped straight out of a Paul Durcan poem. He follows in the Irish bardic tradition – wise man and performer, story-teller and confessor.

We have this reciprocal understanding with Leonard. He brings us the Paraclete, the Saviour's breath, the Belsen heap and we bring the comradeship of the fellow traveller.

~

In late summer 2014, Angela and I set off for the Greek Islands on our honeymoon. The plan had been to island hop but, once we reached Hydra, the hopping stopped. We did visit Spetses and Poros but the quietness of Hydra – no cars, no motorcycles, no bicycles – was enthralling.

The idea had been to visit for a day or two, see some of the sights associated with Leonard's time there and then move on. Instead, we spent the full two weeks walking the island.

One evening, as we made our way back from the beach at sunset, we stopped to admire the view from a headland between Vlichos and Hydra town. We asked two women who were passing whether they would take our photo. They did. As we chatted, they asked if this was our first time on the island. We said it was and enquired if they were regular visitors. One of the women, Maureen, told us she'd been coming to Hydra for years and staying in the Four Corners quarter.

'Ah, Leonard Cohen country,' I said, knowing his house was in that part of Hydra town.

The women nodded and then we parted company.

The following morning, as we breakfasted near the harbour, the two women approached us again.

Angela invited them to join us for coffee.

'It's a small island,' Maureen said, 'you meet everyone several times a day if you spend any time on the waterfront.'

'That's a good thing,' Angela said, 'small town life.'

The coffees arrived.

'I just wanted to say,' Maureen laughed, 'about Four Quarters and Leonard. We're actually staying in his house. Adam is my son-in-law.'

We chatted a little about the connection between Leonard and the island and then went our separate ways.

The following evening, our last on the island, we met a friend for dinner and the next morning made our way down to the harbour to catch the early ferry back to Athens. As we waited to board, Maureen and her friend – they, too, were catching the ferry – joined us in the queue.

'Small town or not,' Maureen said, 'we searched all over for you two last night but we couldn't find you. We thought you might have liked to come up and visit Leonard's house. I know you've been to see it and we thought you might like to actually visit. But we just couldn't find you.'

Hearing Leonard sing 'Song of Bernadette' and visiting Leonard's house – some things are just not meant to be.

~

When Leonard's birthday came around in September, I wrote to him. He was eighty years old and I wanted to tell him how important his work and his friendship had been over the years and how inspiring his writing had been. I felt blessed to have someone with his grace and vision moving ahead of me through the world, readying me for some of the experiences that lay ahead.

I sent a poem I had written for him:

A haiku for Leonard

May your shadow stretch

as strong across the decades

and as kindly, too.

~

The following day, September 22, 2014, *Popular Problems* was released. There were two songs on the album that resonated immediately with me – 'Did I Ever Love You' and 'You Got Me Singing.'

The complication of 'Did I Ever Love You' is there in the title – the uncertainty in the narrative voice – the absolute honesty yet hesitation inherent in that ambiguity. The image of the couple leaning across the old table suggests an association that may have run through years and decades. And the passage, yet stasis, of time, seen in the blossoming of the lemon trees and the withering of the almond trees, is beautifully communicated. The song comes, like a long sigh of acceptance and resignation. It's a life story, told alternately in the slow, world-weary voice of Leonard and the hell for leather, country shades of the Webb sisters. When Leonard asks whether it was ever settled you just know there is no answer to that question, nor ever will be. The asking is in itself a statement of the unsettled nature of the relationship.

It seemed, yet again, that Leonard had written the story of much of my life, years drifting in and out of relationships – and marriages – without ever finding within myself the strength to be the person I wanted to be.

The movement from the wretchedness in Leonard's delivery to the helter-skelter of the Webbs is astonishing, from heartbreak to manic heartbeat and back again – just like life. The questions asked in the song were the ones I had asked myself again and again across the years: was I capable of love or love forever; were things ever settled when relationships ended; what was the purpose of all the nights spent arguing or chatting across a variety of kitchen tables when the outcome always seemed to be the same – failure?

As I was writing this, I went back and listened again to the song and there was a line I had missed in all the hearings – about it being spring and summer, yet *winter forever*.

'Did I Ever Love You' is one of Leonard's simplest yet most complex, plainest yet most quietly alarming songs. It still brings me to the edge of tears.

The closing track on *Popular Problems* was 'You Got Me Singing.' If ever a song cries out for hope and optimism and love in the face of disaster and the suicidal road humanity is travelling, this is it.

And, when Leonard writes about his wish that his *little love* would last, there is nothing little in that dream. It's the hope we all live with and for. The hope, as Raymond Carver writes in 'Late Fragment' that we might be blessed with love and be beloved on this earth. The song – in its anticipation – reminded me of Pete Seeger's equally beautiful and heart-warming 'Rainbow Race.

~

On the day that *Popular Problems* was released, a mail arrived from Leonard:

Dear John

Thank you for your haiku, and for that great piece you wrote for Live in Dublin.

You have always been so very kind and encouraging.

I want you to know how much I appreciate it.

It's two in the morning, been a rough month, and I've kind of run out of steam;

don't have the words to express my deep gratitude, but, believe me, it is there

Much love to you and Angela

L

There was a melancholy in those words that mirrored 'Did I Ever Love You'; a presentiment of darkness, particularly coming, as they did, on the day when his latest album had been released. I remember reading the mail and picturing Leonard sitting at his kitchen table in his little house on South Tremaine. Not quite four in the morning but a silent and obviously bleak hour.

I wrote back, telling him we were thinking of him and hoping the months ahead would be better and that his energy would return. Leonard had always been a very private person and I respected his privacy. I also valued greatly the fact that he had taken the time to write so personally and so candidly. It was obvious from the letter that he was unwell but just how unwell I had no idea.

~

A month later I sent Leonard a copy of my novel, *Joseph*, which had just been published. He replied:

dear bro

deeply touched by your dedication

congratulations on Joseph.

(I know how hard it is to deliver one of these)

very happy for you, John

love and blessings

Leonard

That Christmas I wrote wishing him peace, health, happiness and a bunch of songs in 2015. I also mentioned how wonderful a season Christmas is, that great confluence of Judaism and Christianity.

Leonard's reply, on Christmas Eve, was a living example of what I had in mind:

Thank you, dear John, for your good wishes

and for all your kindness.

May The Christos be born in every heart.

May the Lord bless you and keep you.

May the Lord make his face to shine upon you,

and be gracious to you.

May the Lord lift up his countenance upon you,

and give you peace.

Keep warm, you and your family.

Love,

L

~

Early in 2015 I had an approach from an editor asking me to contact Leonard about a possible contribution to a publication. I also wondered, having been at Leonard's Manchester exhibition, whether a show of Leonard's art work might attract an audience in Ireland. I felt it would.

John,

The old vehicle has sprung a few leaks.

In and out of the shop these days

I'll pass your letter on to Michael Petit.

He can arrange an exhibition.

Don't know if I have a poem.

I'll look around.

You've been so helpful to me over the years.

I hope you know how grateful I am.

Love and Blessings,

L

The weariness was palpable.

Michael Petit is Leonard's graphic designer and curator of Leonard's fine art exhibitions and he got in touch to say he thought an exhibition would be a wonderful idea. Michael had been to Kilkenny, one of the sites I had in mind for an exhibition, and had happy memories of the city.

Over the following months I made approaches to four galleries, in four different cities and towns, but none had an interest in staging an exhibition. One director named another well-known entertainer and said: 'If we had an exhibition of Leonard's work, we'd find ourselves having to exhibit that person's work.' The comparison made no sense but the director then heaped irony on insult by wondering whether I might ask Leonard to consider doing a reading in their exhibition space. I politely declined on his behalf.

~

On September 7, 2015, two weeks before his eighty-first birthday I wrote to Leonard. I had just seen the heart-breaking photographs of Alan Kurdi whose two-year old body had been washed up on the Turkish shore. The sickness and despondency I felt on seeing the images took me back to one of Leonard's darkest works on the *Songs of Love and Hate* album, 'Avalanche.'

The lines about it being a long way down, a sad way down seemed bitterly appropriate when placed beside the photographs. The images of Alan Kurdi, the depth of Leonard's song and the sometimes parlous state of the human race poured into my letter, balanced, somewhat, by memories of better days:

I looked back over twenty years and saw the end of a marriage, the death of an only brother but then I saw the start of a wonderful new marriage; the births of some nieces and nephews; a honeymoon on Hydra this time last year and friendships that continue and deepen, your own among them. And I thought of all of us, smiling, hopeful souls moving every onward....

~

A month later, on October 22, a mail arrived wishing me a happy birthday. Again, it was imbued with that wry sense of humour that was so much a part of Leonard and that, sadly, so many people missed:

dear bro
I warned you about this
but you keep getting older and older
happy birthday, John
love and gratitude
thank you for remembering
the old ways
Leo

The letter reminded me of my brother who had died at the age I had then reached – he was the only other person ever to call me *bro* and he, too, was a good and kind man. His doctoring was of the body; Leonard's was of the heart and mind.

That New Year's Eve a note came from Leonard:

Keep warm.
Keep dry.
Peaceful new year to us all.
See you down the road.
L

~

Back in 1984, my daughter, Lydia, had been with me at my first meeting with Leonard and now, in the summer of 2016, she was about to be married to her fiancé, Brendan Garrett.

A message arrived for their wedding day.

Dear Lydia and Brendan,

I am so happy to learn that you have found one another.

May all the blessings that life has to offer, may all these blessings be yours.

With love from your old friend,

Leonard

~

When I read the letter Leonard had sent to Marianne Ihlen, like so many others, I was touched by its beauty, its love and its gentleness. I sent him a copy of Adrian Mitchell's beautiful, powerful and life-affirming poem 'Death is smaller than I thought.' It seemed to strike a chord:

Thanks for that poem, John.

Nails it.

Love,

L

~

That summer was a strange one. For the third time in two years, we got news of the death of a teenage friend. Beginning in 2013 with a road accident and continuing through the three following summers with deaths by suicide, four teenage boys whom we'd known had died.

The fourth death, by suicide, left me bewildered, angry and

despairing. I could clearly see what the losses had done to those left behind – the anguish, the uncertainty, the desperation were profound. How, I wondered, could any parent come to terms with this parade of slaughter?

As with so many things in my life, the only way I could deal with these events was to write something that might, in some tiny way, acknowledge not just the dead but also the living, still walking in the shadows of the departed. I thought of Leonard and his music and I thought of the great tradition of the sung requiem Mass. And I thought of Nancy Challies, the subject of Leonard's song, 'Seems So Long Ago, Nancy.' She had taken her own life. And I thought of Leonard's young Spanish guitar teacher. He, too, had taken his own life.

I wrote to Leonard, explaining the reason and outlining my idea. His initial response was, *You're an agnostic Quaker, I'm a Jewish Buddhist, how are we supposed to write a Catholic Mass?* I explained that my upbringing was as a Catholic, that I had considered the priesthood as a career at one point and had spent five years in a junior seminary. I had a clear idea but I needed Leonard's approval and responses as we went.

Over the following months I listened to everything he had written and I read and re-read *Book of Mercy* – it seemed the ideal source for the spoken word. Little by little the Mass took shape. Given the background, I suggested *Between Your Love and Mine* as a title.

Coincidentally, a priest friend had just gone through a dark night of the soul – or two years of darkness of the soul – before leaving the priesthood. He had spoken to me about the challenges of those two years: of leading services; administering to the sick and dying; conducting baptisms and blessings and, all the while, not having faith himself. I wanted to include that experience as part of the Mass, a celebrant who must support a couple whose child has died while not believing in any of the words he speaks.

Versions of the Mass bounced back and forth until we were both happy with the finished script. The plan was to premiere the work the following year, 2017, and the hope was that Leonard would be well enough to attend.

~

For Leonard's eighty-second birthday I sent him a copy of Frederic William Burton's beautifully vibrant painting *The Meeting on the Turret Stairs*. In the painting, Hellelil, dressed in a luminous blue dress, meets her personal guard, Hildebrand, on the turret stairs. The couple are in love but the love is secret. As they pass, Hildebrand kisses the sleeve of Hellelil's dress – the kiss has been described as 'a sacrament.' There is something hopelessly propitious in the painting – it is the secret life of which Leonard had written.

He replied the same day:

thank you, John

for good wishes and the painting (like the rest of us, he doesn't know what he's getting into) love

L

~

On October 19 I had a short mail from Leonard. It read:

dear John,

anything you need of mine that you can use, you are very welcome to

love

L

I knew he was referring to *Between Your Love and Mine*, in case there were any last minute changes that might need to be made, I didn't read any more into the letter. Three days later, on my sixty-fourth birthday, another email arrived.

It transpired that Leonard had asked Angela to remind him of the date and, in doing so, she had mentioned that I had been humming the Beatles 'When I'm Sixty-four' for weeks.

The e mail had a wonderful attachment, a short film of Leonard's beloved hummingbird…that sense of humour again. The message read:

and you are 64 years old

Happy birthday, dear friend

Love and blessings,

leonard

~

A day earlier, Leonard's album, *You Want It Darker*, had been released.

'Treaty' immediately seized my attention – that blend of the human and the divine; that melding of the Jewish and the Christian; a fusion of belief and loss of faith; the snake that might not only have slithered out of Eden but might, too, have made its way from D.H. Lawrence's poem. Part of the wealth of Leonard's work, part of the genius of the man was his ability to make the personal universal and to make his vision our vision. Nothing was ever singular in his writing: the influences were multiple, the references were manifold; the meanings were many. Like all great writing, the text of a Cohen song opened itself to the experience of the listener while drawing on the experience of the writer.

And when Leonard sang about being angry and tired it was clear that this was not simply a performance. These words, those notes, that emotion were coming from the heart and soul of a dying man who was filled with a longing and love of life and living.

'Travelling Light' was the other song with which I immediately connected and the accompanying video, with its images of Leonard on the veranda of his home in South Tremaine, joking with Adam; of the younger Leonard striding through life and, then, that last image of the dying man walking slowly down the path in front of his house, his body casting a fading shadow before he pauses, turns and looks back achingly, one last time, left me in no doubt about this being an end.

Fourteen

Angela woke me in the early hours of that Friday morning with the news that our friend was dead. And then the sun rose, as it always does, into a cold and glorious morning. And that, too, seemed appropriate.

Through the years Leonard was always there – the older, wiser man moving on ahead, experiencing life and its losses and gains and sending backs reports in his songs and poems and prayers.

One of the things I loved most about him was his lack of pretence. He was an extraordinarily private person and yet he opened his heart and soul in his work. He was a genius, yet his humility was deep and real. This was the man who queued with the crew for food at gigs; this was the mostly reclusive man who cooked and shopped for himself and shared a modest house on South Tremaine. The humility and honesty that filled the songs were there in his life, in his beliefs and there, too, in his willingness to not hide, not pretend, not be the persona but always the person.

There were profoundly sombre times in Leonard's life: the years when CBS refused to release his work in the United States; the years when his savings disappeared; the more darkly and deeply painful personal depressions. But always the work went on. And always, always – in the songs, in the poems and in the letters – there was a glint in the eye.

The sun rose on that Friday morning with fire and passion, with beauty and warmth, a reminder of the array of gifts that were his to all of us. By then he had been buried in Montreal, buried without fuss or notice, he left as he had lived, with style and grace and humility.

~

The summer after Leonard's death, we premiered *Between Your Love and Mine*. Aisling Carter had come on board as Musical Director the previous autumn, brilliantly arranging the songs. In the spring we began rehearsals with Aisling on piano; Meadbh Farrell and Lucy Deegan playing cellos; Annie Rose Deegan on violin; Dave Day as percussionist and singers Eric Butler; Katie Jacques and Shane Sullivan. The readings from *Book of Mercy* were by Angela Keogh and myself; lighting was by Tom Kennedy and sound by Paul Donohue and Chris Jacques. Geert van der Wijk kindly allowed the use of two of his stunning photographs of Leonard for the programme.

The songs used in the Mass were: 'String Reprise'(Overture); 'Come Healing' (Opening hymn); 'The Faith' (Penitential Act); 'Heart With No Companion' (Kyrie Eleison); 'Nightingale' (Gloria); 'Whither Thou Goest' (Psalm); 'Treaty' (Alleluia); 'Going Home' (Sung Response) 'If I Didn't Have Your Love' (Creed); 'Anthem' (Holy, Holy, Holy); 'Amen' (Great Amen); 'If It Be Your Will' (Sign of Peace); 'Love Itself' (Communion Hymn); 'Song of Bernadette' (Song of Reflection) and 'You Got Me Singing' (Closing Hymn).

The premiere was at the George Bernard Shaw Theatre at VISUAL Carlow on June 15, 2017 and President Michael D Higgins and the Canadian ambassador, Kevin Vickers, were among the audience in a full house. The silence that greeted the last note of the closing song was absolute and intense. Leonard had written once that the standing ovation transcends the whole critical establishment. I wished he were there to hear the silence which transcended applause to be followed, a few moments later, by sustained appreciation and the standing ovation. I was proud but, mostly, I was sorry that Leonard wasn't there to see and hear the response to his work

Backstage, I thanked President Higgins for attending and told him I hoped we had done Leonard proud.

The following morning, I received a call from Áras an Uachtaráin, wondering whether we would be free to present *Between Your Love and Mine* there on Culture night, Friday, September 22 – the night after Leonard's birthday. We were free.

~

That summer we toured *Between Your Love and Mine* to theatres across the country – each performance sold out. And then it was September and the requiem was staged at the Áras. As the applause died away, President Higgins joined the cast on stage. As ever, he was eloquent and astute in noting the fact that the Requiem was by Leonard and for those who had lost and been lost.

'I think your applause has shown how you appreciated this wonderful tribute by Leonard Cohen. When I saw it in VISUAL first, down in Carlow, I was absolutely struck by the sheer beauty and integrity of it and I just want to say, again, what a marvellous, marvellous presentation and how fortunate we were that they were willing and able to reassemble themselves and come to Áras an Uachtaráin as the contribution of Sabina and myself to Culture Night.

'I just want to say how very, very, very grateful I am to John MacKenna and all the musicians and the great voices we heard and, indeed, how grateful we are to Leonard Cohen who lit up so many lives all around the world and very particularly when he came to Ireland.

'I want to thank all of you for coming along, I hope you've had a wonderful evening and if you want to take the opportunity to visit the house, you're very, very welcome. And all I can say is go safely home to where it is better than before.'

Again, I was proud but saddened that Leonard wasn't there to see and hear the words of the President and the heartfelt response of the audience.

~

On what would have been Leonard's eighty-fifth birthday, September 21, 2019, we staged *Between Your Love and Mine* at the National Concert Hall as part of a short, six-venue tour.

In an article for the *Irish Times*, I outlined the background to the writing and staging of the requiem. As I wrote, I was very aware of the added poignancy of performing the work after Leonard's death:

The procession of young deaths and the heroic efforts of those left behind, set me thinking about how to respond and, eventually, about the possibility of creating a work for stage that would reflect the bewilderment and anguish felt by family and friends. A requiem seemed the obvious answer, a requiem Mass. But where and how to start?

I emailed Leonard Cohen, a friend of 30 years, and asked whether, together, we might create such a work.

Over the following weeks, I outlined my idea in greater detail: a requiem for stage, shaped on the liturgy of the Mass but using only Leonard's words and music to create that liturgy. I had spent days and nights listening and re-listening to his songs and reading through his books – in particular, Book of Mercy. I sent him an outline of what I had in mind and, over the following months, the emails came and went with suggestions and recommendations. Leonard sent me a poem I hadn't seen before. The text began to take shape, as did the central roles of the mother and father of the dead child and the celebrant who, in spite of his loss of faith, must celebrate this final, heartbreakingly important Mass.

It seemed to me that Leonard's music and words were ideal for these subjects: his work is littered with religious and spiritual imagery; with hope and sanguinity, and yet it's also strewn with doubt, human weakness and uncertainty.

One morning, two weeks later, my wife, Angela, woke me before six. 'Leonard is gone,' she said. She had heard the news on the radio. I turned on my phone. Already there were texts from my friends Joe Taylor and Rob Canning.

Suddenly, the importance of staging the requiem took on a new urgency. What had been a requiem by Leonard became also, in an unexpected way, a requiem for Leonard.

Drawing together a group of musicians and singers to perform the requiem proved easier than I had imagined. I wanted a team from the immediate area and, with the help of Mary Amond O'Brien and Majella Swan, directors of music schools in Carlow, and with recommendations from Aisling Carter, we assembled a cast: three lead singers, two cellists, a violinist, a percussion player and a pianist, all under Aisling's musical direction. The addition of two actors completed the onstage crew and rehearsals began that spring. Meanwhile, lighting technician Tom Kennedy set about designing a lighting plan that would create the onstage atmosphere for the requiem.

The stage set was simplicity itself: a rough kitchen table (made by our drummer, David Day, from old boards and the remnants of a timber ladder) was reflective of the table at which the couple sit in their suddenly silent house and of the altar table at which the requiem Mass will be sung. A kitchen chair on each side, some flowers, a teapot, two cups (one of which doubles as a chalice), a book and a bunch of wild flowers complete the table setting. The starkness of the story, the beauty of the music and the power of the singing tell the rest.

The closing of the requiem was the most challenging part: how to leave the audience with a sense of the depth of the suffering endured by families, while, at the same time, lifting the spirit to a sense of hope, a reminder that life continues – radically altered but even more important now – for those who remain. In the end we settled on one of Leonard's lesser-known songs, 'You Got Me Singing.' The lyrics seemed particularly apposite.

The response was overpowering: from those who had lost sons and daughters; from those who were dealing with the trauma of suicide in their families; from those who had loved Leonard and his work and felt his loss as they might that of a family member.

The sadness, love, hurt, compassion, uncertainty and redemptive power of Leonard's words and music struck a communal chord with audiences across the country. And then the short tour ended, but the work remained.

Late last year, I contacted Leonard's family and his manager, Robert Kory, and suggested a restaging of the work on Leonard's 85th birthday, September 21st, 2019. It seemed an appropriate celebration of the occasion and the man. They agreed.

In revisiting the script, I added a short prelude, drawing further on Leonard's work, amplifying the sense of agnosticism in the character of the celebrant and 'the panic of loss' in the figures of the bereaved parents. In doing that, I became conscious of the shadows of my own parents in the wings – they lost three children to stillbirth, and, given the mores of the time, the babies were buried at the bottom of our garden, the gates of Christian cemeteries being closed to unbaptised children.

To my delight, all of the original cast and crew are available for the NCH staging and the other five performances, and we have added three further singers, deepening the sense of community in the requiem. Artist Siobhán Jordan has created a tapestry for the lectern used on stage, based on a design by Leonard.

But, most of all, this work is about three things: reflecting on the loss of parents whose children have accidentally or intentionally stepped out of this life; facing the loss of faith many people experience, even those tasked with supporting communities who, in a time of crisis, seek the succour of belief; and, now, remembering the man who created this beautiful music and these beautiful words and whose generosity made the requiem possible.

~

The National Concert Hall performance was an extraordinarily affecting one. The cast and crew were joined on the night by Aspiro Choir founder Mary Amond-O'Brien and three singers from the choir: Aimee Andrews, Cillian Dooley and Clare Miller.

In the audience were Robert and Phyllis Kory. Robert was and is Leonard's manager and he joined us on the stage of the NCH and spoke about Leonard and the requiem.

'This is a truly magnificent work and it's a delight for me to be here to celebrate Leonard's birthday with you. A very busy birthday … but there's no place I'd rather be than with you here this evening because this is a work which will enable Leonard's work to continue for generations.

'So what would Leonard have me say? First of all, he'd like me to thank John for plumbing the depths of his work as an artist, his poetry, his music and his songs to create a new work which can live in its own right.

'He'd also like me to thank the musicians for your extraordinary skill in playing and particularly the drummer, such quiet…Leonard told me that such drummers are all but impossible to find. And he'd also like me to thank the performers and those who did the readings for truly making Leonard's work your own because, in that way, you bring it to life in a whole new way.

'So, I thank you.'

As Robert spoke, my eye fell on an empty seat in the third row of the hall, one empty seat. Perhaps tonight, I thought, perhaps tonight that seat was occupied by the spirit of my absent friend. And I smiled.

Two months later, on November 22 2019, Leonard's posthumous album, *Thanks for the Dance*, was released. He was gone but, as promised, we were hearing from him.

The album was a thirty-minute autobiographical epistle in nine chapters on living, love and dying.

Opening with 'Happens to the Heart,' it celebrates the brightness of Leonard's dying fire. The song, as he says, is a revisiting of the things that happened to his heart across a lifetime.

'Moving On' continues the evocative journey with a bitter twist in the tale. Who's moving? Wistfully, Leonard answers: Who's kidding who? His consciousness of the stranger on the stair is palpable.

'The Night of Santiago' is a last homage to Lorca, a version of Lorca's poem 'La Casada Infiel' (The Unfaithful Wife). In an interview with Apple music, Adam Cohen, who produced the album and wrote much of the music, said: 'I'd heard it under construction for years, on the front lawn or while we were having coffee or dinner, and I'd always begged him to attempt to write music to it. In a weakened state, he said: "Look, I'll just recite the poem to a certain tempo and you go ahead and write the music and try to tell the story.'

I had long hoped Leonard would record 'Thanks for the Dance' (which had first appeared on Anjani Thomas' album *Blue Alert*) and there it was as the title track on the final CD. The song is a hymn to loss and forgiveness, a song that recalls and speculates without claiming to have any answers.

'It's Torn' is a dark exposition of life, the world, the spiritual, the personal and the person – ending with an observation of great empathy, that there are untruths in the things we believe to be holy and veracities in the many things that are often dishonest.

'The Goal' offers a sad and beautiful picture of Leonard settling accounts in his dying days. And when he refers in the song to the fall – that storied Old Testament event – there is, too, given the manner of his dying, a certain prescience in the image. As I listen, I'm there observing Leonard share a smile – but one of surrender – with his passing neighbour. And yet, and yet, and yet there's the echo of his warning from thirty years earlier about charismatic holy men – there's no one to follow – and also that potent Zen reminder that by setting goals we are, in fact, limiting ourselves and our possibilities. What a breath-taking philosophy to carry through this life and into eternity.

'Puppets' differs from anything else in this final, farewell letter. It's a scathing elucidation of the political and the social exploitation and abuse and murder of people across the generations and it's a questioning of just how much – or how little – control we have over our own lives, a point that's particularly salient in the face of death.

'The Hills' is a deeply honest and painful exploration, a pulling back of the curtain to reveal the face of death. Nevertheless, there is hope, optimism even, in the lines where Leonard recognises the brief crossing of paths, less than a second, when, as he leaves, someone else (a female figure) will arrive into the world to complete the things he couldn't do. It's a moment of immense belief and resolution. The longing in the song is intense but so, too, is the sense of anticipation.

The epistle closes with 'Listen to the Hummingbird' – a note on the brevity of life and an urging of the listener not to pay heed to Leonard's words but to listen, instead, to the natural teachers and to the mind of God.

Those last words in this wonderful, posthumous missive are, unsurprisingly, ones of humility, modesty and self-effacement.

~

As I listen, again and again, to that closing dispatch I frequently think of the words Leonard spoke from the stage on his final tour: "May you be surrounded by family and friends, and if this is not your lot, may the blessings find you in your solitude.'

Amen, brother, amen.

Acknowledgements

My sincere thanks to my sister, Dolores MacKenna, and the late Margaret Leahy for introducing me to Leonard's work; to Robert Kory, Robert Canning, John Scally, Lucy Deegan, Theo Dorgan, Jerome Taheny, Jarkko Arjatsalo, Gerard Smyth, Colm Walsh, Brid Brophy, Faye Tucker and Mark Turner for their help and encouragement.

And a particular thanks to Leonard Cohen for his comradeship, inspiration and generosity – may the blessings find you, too, my friend.

A playlist of songs mentioned in the book.

So long Marianne
Bird on the wire
The Partisan
Hey that's no way to say goodbye
Avalanche
Dress rehearsal rag
Famous blue raincoat
Kevin Barry
Take this longing
There is a war
The guests
Ballad of the absent mare
Hallelujah
First we take Manhattan
I'm your man
Tower of song
Whither thou goest
Please don't pass me by
The future
Tacoma trailer
In my secret life

Suzanne
Story of Isaac
Tonight will be fine
Chelsea Hotel
Last year's man
Diamonds in the mine
Joan of Arc
A singer must die
Who by fire
True love leaves no traces
Our Lady of solitude
Dance me to the end of love
If it be your will
Song of Bernadette
Take this waltz
Sisters of mercy
Passing through
Seems so long ago, Nancy
Light as the breeze
Waiting for the miracle
Love itself

Alexandra leaving

The faith

Undertow

Lover, lover, lover

Going home

Come healing

Did I ever love you

Treaty

String reprise

Nightingale

Happens to the heart

The night of Santiago

It's torn

Puppets

Listen to the hummingbird

So, we'll go no more a roving

Everybody knows

Night comes on

Crazy to love you

Amen

Save the last dance for me

You got me singing

Traveling light

Heart with no companion

If I didn't have your love

Moving on

Thanks for the dance

The goal

The hills

A reading list of Leonard's publications mentioned in the book

The Favourite Game

Book of Mercy

The Flame

Beautiful losers

Book of Longing